MEDLINE

FOR HEALTH PROFESSIONALS

HOW TO SEARCH

PubMed

ON THE INTERNET

David Hutchinson, RN

MEDLINE for Health Professionals: How to Search PubMed on the Internet

Copyright © October 1998 David Hutchinson
    dbhutchinson@ucdavis.edu

Graphic Design by Stornetta Publications
    storneta@ix.netcom.com
    http://www.stornetta.com/

Cataloging Data

David Hutchinson

    MEDLINE® for Health Professionals: How to Search PubMed® on the Internet —1st ed.
    Includes index.
    ISBN 0-9651412-6-8

New Wind Publishing
Box 161613
Sacramento, CA 95816-1613
916.451.9039
http://NewWindPub.com
info@NewWindPub.com

Limits of Liability and Disclaimer of Warranty

Trademarks and Copyright

Printed in the United States of America

10 9 8 7 6 5 4 3 2 1

ALSO BY DAVID HUTCHINSON, RN

- *The Internet Workbook for Health Professionals*, 1997
- *A Pocket Guide to the Medical Internet, Second Edition,* 1997
- *A Tale of Two Kitties,* 1996
- *An Internet Guide for the Health Professional, Second Edition,* 1996 (with Michael Hogarth, MD)

About the Author

David Hutchinson, RN, BSN, received his BA in Physics from Kenyon College in 1976 and his BSN from the University of Arizona College of Nursing in 1986. For eight years he worked as a pediatric nurse at the UC Davis Medical Center, achieving an Excellence in Nursing award. In 1994 he began to work with computers, and is now involved in many aspects of that work: creation and maintenance of a Web site; teaching several classes, including MEDLINE; writing handouts; installation and trouble-shooting; network maintenance. He contributes regularly to journals, and speaks to professional groups, nursing schools, and healthcare organizations. He is also a devoted father of two cats, Scotty and Athena.

About New Wind Publishing

New Wind specializes in books about the medical Internet.

Acknowledgments

Thanks are due to the many people who read through the manuscript and gave helpful suggestions: Ken Ratter, Terri Malmgren, Ann Sievers, Mary Jane Sauvé, Joe and Emma Gunterman, John Ward, Floyd Dunn, Peggy Wetsch, and Lawrence McGrath. Their contributions have helped to clear the cobwebs from my thinking and made the book better able to serve the professionals for whom it is intended.

The many people at the NLM should be noted for their excellent training materials and continued efforts to provide medical information for professionals and the public. Thanks to Caroline Tilley for her detailed critique.

Most of all I would like to thank Frank Norman, who provided invaluable comments and pointed out multiple places where the manuscript needed improvement. Through his astute observations he reminded me that we need librarians more than ever to navigate and survive in this information-saturated world.

TYPOGRAPHIC CONVENTIONS

Text which you should type is shown in `Courier font`.

Areas or buttons in PubMed such as Advanced Search or Display are shown in **bold**.

Internet addresses are shown in bold italic:
http://www.ncbi.nlm.nih.gov/PubMed.

Titles of books and journals are italicized: *New England Journal of Medicine*.

True acronyms such as MEDLARS are in upper case.

Letters of words which form acronyms are underlined when explained: <u>M</u>edical <u>A</u>nalysis and <u>R</u>etrieval <u>S</u>ystem.

Screen captures have a box around them to differentiate the screen image clearly:

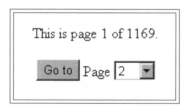

Screen capture

TABLE OF CONTENTS

APPENDICES

1 INTRODUCTION

A NEW LANDSCAPE

We live in changing times. Not too long ago a library was simply a repository for books and journals neatly arranged on stacks, with a card catalog in the corner. As computer databases developed in the sixties and seventies, catalogs became automated, and searching took on a different character. Imagine, typing a word to find a book rather than leafing through cards or walking the stacks! Then in the eighties the Internet was born, and in the nineties it developed, touching every aspect of culture — especially those vast repositories of knowledge, libraries.

The role of librarian has also been changing. Information professionals don't pace through dusty corridors; they're likely to be found working on sophisticated Web sites or databases such as Online Mendelian Inheritance in Man (OMIM), a database of genes and genetic disorders. As access to knowledge has expanded, so has the importance of their role in helping to organize the wide range of resources available. If your notion of looking for a book is to wander the stacks, or if you think that the best way to find an article is to glance through one or two journals, you need to talk to a librarian.

Our children are growing up with the sing-song of fax machines and modems as they talk daily with people from around the world using the instantaneous magic of the Internet. If you are one of the paper generation, it isn't easy to accept this new world. A friend of mine took five years deciding to buy a fax, and he's still pondering the advantages and disadvantages of the Internet. Health professionals, facing endless complexities of hardware and software, often avoid computers. The tragedy is that these are the very tools which can help us in our practice!

With the advent of the World Wide Web, searching a database is easier than ever before. Many library catalogs have online forms which can be used by children. The Internet itself has become the largest public-access library of information in the world, and millions of people are searching and finding information, especially medical information, on the Internet.

But even though there are tremendous health resources available on the Internet, the single most important source for authoritative medical information is MEDLINE. MEDLINE has a thesaurus and hierarchy (MeSH) of more than 18,000 terms which organizes the database conceptually, and more than forty separate fields which qualify each citation. With that degree of organization, MEDLINE offers health professionals an unsurpassed research tool. You can search it for free on the World Wide Web. This book will show you how.

WHAT IS MEDLINE?

MEDLINE is a computerized card catalog for medical journals. Maintained by the National Library of Medicine (NLM) in Bethesda, Maryland, MEDLINE is a *bibliographic* or *citation* database, meaning that it has citations to literature. It gives access to *authoritative, published* medical articles. (There is a huge supply of medical information on the Internet, but much of it is neither formally published nor does it undergo the peer review process typical of professional publications.)

MEDLINE is the most comprehensive database for health and medicine; it includes citations to articles from more than 3,900 journals around the world. The complete database covers literature from 1966 to the present, for a total of nine million individual references. More than 80% of the articles are in English. It does not contain the full text of articles, but 75% of the citations have abstracts (short summaries). Chapter 9 explains how to obtain an article (via mail, fax, or email) using the Loansome Doc service of the NLM.

WHY SHOULD PROFESSIONALS USE MEDLINE?

Several studies show that using MEDLINE directly affects patient care. A 1993 article in the *Journal of the American Medical Association* (1993;269:3124-9) found that 41% of all MEDLINE searches affected diagnoses, tests, or treatments of patients. Another (*Academic Medicine*, 1994 Jun;69(6):489-495) demonstrates that costs, charges, and length of stay can be reduced by using MEDLINE early in a patient's hospitalization. An article from the *Bulletin of the Medical Library Association* (1992;80:169-178) estimated that 80% of physicians felt the information they received from medical librarians affected the way they managed patients. Finally, if students are taught to use MEDLINE and given assignments in using it frequently, they will continue to use it later in their careers (*Academic Medicine*, 1994 Nov;69(11):914-920). Because learning to use MEDLINE is a skill that should be practiced and done well, Chapters 7 and 8 give exercises and strategies.

COPYRIGHT

The National Library of Medicine allows redistribution (reprinting) of "small" amounts of information from its various databases. Small means "approximately 1,000 records per month." Allowable information for redistribution includes the bibliographic citations and MeSH terms, but it does not cover the abstract. Individual authors write abstracts; copyright permission to use them must be obtained directly from authors or publishers.

WHAT YOU WON'T FIND IN MEDLINE

Many questions are not suited to a MEDLINE search. Health professionals go through a dizzying amount of information in a working day, very little of which will be found in the latest journal. "What is the correct dose for this medication?" "Who do I refer this patient to?" Basic questions of anatomy and physiology, traditional treatments, standard pharmaceutical information are best answered by going to texts. Procedures often are available in hospital manuals. You consult other professionals by phone, fax, email – as well as use a literature database such as MEDLINE. Remember: use the right source for what you need.

Also, MEDLINE is not all-encompassing, at least not yet. It does not index books, newspaper articles, audio tapes, films, multimedia, computer software, nor does it cover Internet Web sites, mailing lists or newsgroups. To search for these you must go to an appropriate reference or search engine. (If you don't know how to find medical information on the Internet, please see my *Internet Workbook for Health Professionals*).

Although you cannot read the full text of an article directly from MEDLINE, publishers of medical journals are beginning to put full text of some articles on the Internet. In these cases, PubMed links directly to the publisher's site. Currently the number of journals with full text is small (about a hundred) but this number will grow in the future. Just because a journal has text on the Web does not mean that you can read it free of charge; most publishers require some sort of subscription fee or registration for access to their full site.

See Appendix C for links to and methods of finding types of information not covered by MEDLINE.

ACCESS TO MEDLINE

Since mid-1997, MEDLINE has been available for free over the World Wide Web, through a site called PubMed ***http://www.ncbi.nlm.nih.gov/PubMed***. There is no charge for using PubMed, nor are passwords required: it is available to anyone in the world who has access to the Internet.

The MEDLINE database can be leased by institutions, and other programs such as Ovid, Infotrieve, Knowledge Finder, Silverplatter, etc. have been developed to search and access the MEDLINE database. Some university systems, such as the University of California's Melvyl, have their own interface to MEDLINE, so health professionals should ask their librarian if these are available in the local library. Many health-related Web sites offer access to MEDLINE, either for free or after registration. See Appendix C for lists and links to these sites.

To reiterate, PubMed is a computer interface developed by the NLM for searching the MEDLINE database of medical journal citations. Other interfaces search the same database, but have different screens and options.

HOW DIFFICULT IS MEDLINE?

Don't worry. PubMed is not difficult to learn, even the so-called "Advanced Search" screen. The Basic Search page is simple: type a word and click Search. On the advanced search, you can choose a field such as title word, then type your word and search. You do not need to learn a complicated computer language. The basics of searching PubMed can be learned in an hour or two, by working through Chapters 3, 4, and 5.

The skill in using MEDLINE is in narrowing your results. You may get thousands of citations if you search for a general topic. Even though you know what you are looking for – "A recent research article which compares the use of different broad-spectrum antibiotics with iatrogenic infections" – you may be unclear how to find such an article. See Chapter 4 for instructions on doing an advanced search, Chapter 6 for exercises, and Chapter 7 for overall strategies in using PubMed.

To use PubMed well, you should understand:

- how MEDLINE uses the Medical Subject Headings (MeSH) vocabulary

- the different fields (MeSH, publication type, etc.) available for searching

- how to modify a query using the Boolean connectors AND, OR, NOT

PUBMED VERSUS INTERNET GRATEFUL MED

The first choice you have when going to the NLM MEDLINE page is whether to use PubMed or Internet Grateful Med. In this book, I teach only PubMed. I consider PubMed to be better. In general, PubMed is more open-ended in constructing a query, whereas Internet Grateful Med, though simple in some respects, can be restrictive. PubMed offers a more complete range of search options, and is more tailored to the professional. The beginning search screens of PubMed are straightforward:

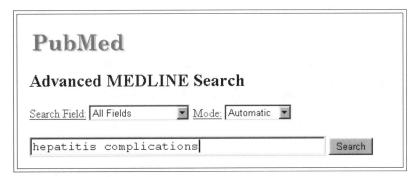

PubMed Advanced Search screen

Grateful Med was originally created as software used to access MEDLINE from a stand-alone computer. However, it is much easier to develop and maintain a Web-based interface than a complete program, so the National Library of Medicine decided to discontinue future upgrades to Grateful Med. In its place they now offer Internet Grateful Med.

Internet Grateful Med is similar in purpose to PubMed: it gives free access to MEDLINE through a series of Web forms. The screens are relatively easy to use, but it can be more difficult to set up complex query.

Here is the basic search screen from Internet Grateful Med:

National Library of Medicine: Internet Grateful Med Search Screen

i   [Perform Search] [Find MeSH/ Meta Terms] [Search Other Files] [Analyze Search] [Specify Journals] [Clear Search] [Log off IGM]

Internet Grateful Med is currently set to search file MEDLINE

i **Enter Query Terms:**

Search for

| | as | Subject ▼ | Add OR |

AND search for

| | as | Subject ▼ | Add OR |

AND search for

| | as | Subject ▼ | Add OR |

i **Apply Limits:**

Languages:	All ▼	**Publ Types:**	All ▼
Study Groups:	All ▼	**Gender:**	All ▼
Age Groups:	All ▼	**Journals:**	All ▼
Year range:	1995 ▼	**Ending Year:**	1998 ▼
Single publication year only: 19	98		

Internet Grateful Med

It is best to choose one program for doing a task, and then stick with it, because it takes time to become familiar with the options and peculiarities of a program. Although Internet Grateful Med has drop-down lists in its beginning screen (publication types, journal subsets, age groups, etc.), the choices in many of these lists are limited. For example, only seven of the roughly fifty publication types are listed, and in the top search boxes you can only choose author, title, or subject.

PubMed's beginning screen is simpler for getting started, and the various displays are less cluttered with custom designed buttons. Because PubMed uses its thesaurus to assign MeSH terms and permits you to connect multiple terms with Boolean AND, you can search quickly using PubMed's single text box. The multiple boxes and choices in Internet Grateful Med are daunting to a beginner.

Finally, PubMed has a number of features that health professionals will find extremely useful, such as the See Related Articles,

Clinical Browser, MeSH Browser, and links to full-text articles on the Internet. PubMed appears to have the most potential for growth as an interface to MEDLINE on the Internet.

Of course, there is much room for improvement in PubMed, and the National Library of Medicine is continually upgrading this resource. Limiting a search to subheadings of a MeSH term can be a confusing process, and modifying a search after starting from the Basic Search screen is difficult.

These are minor criticisms, compared to the ease of getting started, the complex algorithms working behind simple text boxes, and the ability to generate detailed searches. Internet Grateful Med may be useful for some, but for those who plan to use MEDLINE extensively I recommend PubMed.

A lengthy comparison of the features of these two interfaces can be found at

http://www.nnlm.nlm.nih.gov/nnlm/online/pmed-igm.html

A comparison of the features of PubMed and Internet Grateful Med in table form can be found at

http://www.nnlm.nlm.nih.gov/ner/nesl/9707/debate.html

WHAT IS NOT IN THIS BOOK

The world of computers is vast, and even touching on every topic which relates to medical information and computers would double or triple the length of this book. I have also seen that general surveys often leave people with no practical skill or understanding. So this book has one focus: learning to use the PubMed interface to MEDLINE. There are many related subjects which have been left out. If you are new to computers or the Internet and wish to learn about email, the Web, medical directories, searching, and so on, I recommend my recent book, *The Internet Workbook for Health Professionals* (New Wind Publishing). The *Workbook* also contains an extensive bibliography of recent books covering Internet medical topics. The following subjects are *not* covered in this book:

- general computer terms, processes, or use
- PC or mainframe hardware and technical issues
- word processing, spreadsheet, or database programs
- programming languages such as Java, Perl, Cobol, or Fortran
- Internet programs or protocols such as email, Web browsers, ftp, telnet
- Internet search engines such as AltaVista, Lycos, Medical World Search
- Internet medical directories such as Health On the Net, Medical Matrix
- medical informatics or related fields
- clinical information systems, electronic medical records
- telemedicine, virtual reality, voice recognition, and other emerging technologies

WHAT IS IN THIS BOOK

- **Chapter 2** gives a brief introduction to the content of a MEDLINE citation.

- **Chapters 3-5** give a hands-on tutorial to the screens and functions of PubMed.

- **Chapter 6** has step-by-step exercises to practice searching.

- **Chapter 7** has strategies and other tips, to help develop your skills.

- **Chapter 8** explains a few features of PubMed in depth, such as See Related Articles.

- **Chapter 9** outlines how to obtain full-text materials through the document delivery service of the NLM called Loansome Doc.

The appendices give useful background material.

- **Appendix A** explains the history of *Index Medicus* and the NLM, and gives contact information for the NLM and regional libraries.

- **Appendix B** is a short introduction to a few other health-related databases: EMBASE, CINAHL, British Nursing Index, and the Cochrane Library, RNdex, and AMED.

- **Appendix C** gives Internet addresses for many documents, factsheets, and tutorials related to PubMed. It also contains a succinct description and list of Internet resources for types of information that are not available from MEDLINE.

- **Appendix D** contains lists of the MeSH hierarchy, searchable fields, publication types, and two-letter abbreviations.

2 ANATOMY OF A CITATION

DATA IN A MEDLINE CITATION

Just as MEDLINE is much more than just a database, a citation in MEDLINE is more than just an electronic card. In addition to the typical author, title, and subject categories, it has subcategories, information on grants, the type of publication, a unique number (identifier) and more. A basic familiarity with the information in a citation will allow you to construct better, faster, and more efficient searches.

Each citation in MEDLINE is a record, and each record contains many fields. There is an author field, a year field, and so on. (Each field may have more than one entry; for example, there can be twenty-five authors listed for an article.) The original author also writes the abstract, and the publisher sends the basic data - author, title, journal, volume, abstract – to the NLM for inclusion in MEDLINE. NLM staff add additional fields and information such as MeSH terms, date of entry into PubMed, and a Unique Identifier. The citation is then moved from PreMEDLINE to MEDLINE.

The *abstract* field contains a short summary of the article. Abstracts were first included in MEDLINE in 1975, and the percentage of articles with abstracts continues to increase. Approximately 80% of the articles currently in MEDLINE contain abstracts, but this drops to about 50% for citations from the 1970s. In MEDLINE, all abstracts are in English, even if the original article is in another language. You can often learn all you need to know about a specific research study (purpose, methodology, results, conclusions) from an abstract alone.

In the past the National Library of Medicine limited the number of words that could be included in an abstract. At first it was limited to 250 words, then 400 words. Since January 1996 the limit has been removed, but the abstract field will contain only 4,096 characters. If the entire abstract is not present in PubMed, you will see "Abstract truncated at ____ words" at the end.

REPORTS

A report is the format in which a record is printed or displayed on screen. For example, it might be useful to have a brief report showing only the basic information, and another giving everything related to the article. PubMed has four types of reports: the **Document Summary list** (very brief), **Abstract Report**, **Citation Report**, and **MEDLINE Report**.

The information which you first see in the Document Summary list screen is fairly short:

Jones TW, et al.   [See Related Articles]
    Decreased epinephrine responses to hypoglycemia during sleep.
    N Engl J Med. 1998 Jun 4; 338(23): 1657-1662.
    PMID: 9614256; UI: 98264451.

Document list citation

ABSTRACT REPORT

The Abstract Report is most useful for clinical purposes. It gives you all the pertinent information in a form suitable for reading and printing.

N Engl J Med 1998 Jun 4;**338(23):**1657-1662

Decreased epinephrine responses to hypoglycemia during sleep.

Jones TW, Porter P, Sherwin RS, Davis EA, O'Leary P, Frazer F, Byrne G, Stick S, Tamborlane WV

Department of Diabetes and Endocrinology, Princess Margaret Hospital for Children, Perth, WA, Australia.

BACKGROUND: In patients with type I diabetes mellitus, hypoglycemia occurs commonly during sleep and is frequently asymptomatic. This raises the question of whether sleep is associated with reduced counterregulatory-hormone responses to hypoglycemia. METHODS: We studied the counterregulatory-hormone responses to insulin-induced hypoglycemia in eight adolescent patients with type I diabetes and six age-matched normal subjects when they were awake during the day, asleep at night, and awake at night. In each study, the plasma glucose concentration was stabilized for 60 minutes at approximately 100 mg per deciliter (5.6 mmol per liter) and then reduced to 50 mg per deciliter (2.8 mmol per liter) and maintained at that concentration for 40 minutes. Plasma free insulin, epinephrine, norepinephrine, cortisol, and growth hormone were measured frequently during each study. Sleep was monitored by polysomnography. RESULTS: The plasma glucose and free insulin concentrations were similar in both groups during all studies. During the studies when the subjects were asleep, no one was awakened during the hypoglycemic phase, but during the final 30 minutes of the studies when the subjects were awake both the patients with diabetes and the normal subjects had symptoms of hypoglycemia. In the patients with diabetes, plasma epinephrine responses to hypoglycemia were blunted when they were asleep (mean [+/-SE] peak plasma epinephrine concentration, 70+/-14 pg per milliliter [382+/-76 pmol per liter]; P=0.3 for the comparison with base line), as compared with when they were awake during the day or night (238+/-39 pg per milliliter [1299+/-213 pmol per liter] P=0.004 for the comparison with base line, and 296+/-60 pg per milliliter [1616+/-327 pmol per liter], P=0.004, respectively). The patients' plasma norepinephrine responses were also reduced during sleep, whereas their plasma cortisol concentrations did not increase and their plasma growth hormone concentrations increased slightly. The patterns of counterregulatory-hormone responses in the normal subjects were similar. CONCLUSIONS: Sleep impairs counterregulatory-hormone responses to hypoglycemia in patients with diabetes and normal subjects.

PMID: 9614256, UI: 98264451

Abstract report

CITATION REPORT

The Citation Report includes MeSH terms as well as substance names and grant numbers, if they are available. You can use the Citation Report to understand where a particular article falls in the MeSH conceptual hierarchy. Asterisks indicate a MeSH major subject; in effect, these are the main subject(s) of the article. Here is the **additional** information from the Citation Report on the same article. (This report also includes the abstract).

MeSH Terms:

- Adolescence
- Blood Glucose/analysis
- Circadian Rhythm
- Diabetes Mellitus, Insulin-Dependent/blood*
- Epinephrine/blood*
- Female
- Glucose Clamp Technique
- Human
- Hydrocortisone/blood
- Hypoglycemia/chemically induced
- Hypoglycemia/blood*
- Insulin/blood
- Insulin/administration & dosage
- Male
- Norepinephrine/blood
- Reference Values
- Sleep/physiology*
- Somatropin/blood
- Support, Non-U.S. Gov't
- Support, U.S. Gov't, P.H.S.

Substances:

- Epinephrine
- Norepinephrine
- Hydrocortisone
- Somatropin
- Insulin
- Blood Glucose

Grant support:

Additional information in Citation report

MEDLINE REPORT

The MEDLINE Report is more extensive and reveals the hidden structure of the MEDLINE database. In this view, you see the two-letter abbreviation for the field name (what is called the *category qualifier* in MEDLINE). For example AU (author), LA (language), PG (page number), or AB (abstract). There are more than forty different fields of this sort which hold information about an article, although not every citation has an entry for each field. Note that every field allows for a different way to categorize citations in the MEDLINE database, so you can see why it is one of the most important and complex bibliographic databases in the world. See Appendix D for a complete list of these abbreviations.

The MEDLINE Report is used to download results for use in bibliographic software programs such as Reference Manager or ProCite *http://www.risinc.com*, EndNote *http://www.niles.com*, or Papyrus *http://www.teleport.com/~rsd*. These programs store, sort, print, and manage bibliographies. By using the Citation Matcher and the MEDLINE Report from PubMed, you can create a bibliography and avoid the time-consuming and error-prone method of manually typing each one.

The two-letter abbreviations in the MEDLINE Report tell you quite a bit about the article in addition to the standard title, author, and subject. Included are the codes for the International Standard Serial Number (IS), for the journal the country where the article was published (CY), the date of publication (DP), even an address where the research was done. Words in the address field are searchable, so you can use it in a rough way to search for authors associated, for example, with the University of Arizona.

If the article is in a foreign language but includes an abstract in English, the MeSH heading "English Abstract" is added to the citation. This means that an abstract is available in the journal itself, not necessarily in MEDLINE. Below is the MEDLINE Report for the article shown in the Abstract Report above.

```
UI  - 98264451
AU  - Jones TW
AU  - Porter P
AU  - Sherwin RS
AU  - Davis EA
AU  - O'Leary P
AU  - Frazer F
AU  - Byrne G
AU  - Stick S
AU  - Tamborlane WV
TI  - Decreased epinephrine responses to hypoglycemia during sleep.
LA  - Eng
MH  - Adolescence
MH  - Blood Glucose/analysis
MH  - Circadian Rhythm
MH  - Diabetes Mellitus, Insulin-Dependent/*blood
MH  - Epinephrine/*blood
MH  - Female
MH  - Glucose Clamp Technique
MH  - Human
MH  - Hydrocortisone/blood
MH  - Hypoglycemia/*blood/chemically induced
MH  - Insulin/administration & dosage/blood
MH  - Male
MH  - Norepinephrine/blood
MH  - Reference Values
MH  - Sleep/*physiology
MH  - Somatropin/blood
MH  - Support, Non-U.S. Gov't
MH  - Support, U.S. Gov't, P.H.S.
RN  - 0 (Blood Glucose)
RN  - 11061-68-0 (Insulin)
RN  - 12629-01-5 (Somatropin)
RN  - 50-23-7 (Hydrocortisone)
RN  - 51-41-2 (Norepinephrine)
RN  - 51-43-4 (Epinephrine)
PT  - JOURNAL ARTICLE
```

MEDLINE report

```
EM  - 199808
AB  - BACKGROUND: In patients with type I diabetes mellitus, hypoglycemia
      occurs commonly during sleep and is frequently asymptomatic. This
      raises the question of whether sleep is associated with reduced
      counterregulatory-hormone responses to hypoglycemia. METHODS: We
      studied the counterregulatory-hormone responses to insulin-induced
      hypoglycemia in eight adolescent patients with type I diabetes and six
      age-matched normal subjects when they were awake during the day, asleep
      at night, and awake at night. In each study, the plasma glucose
      concentration was stabilized for 60 minutes at approximately 100 mg per
      deciliter (5.6 mmol per liter) and then reduced to 50 mg per deciliter
      (2.8 mmol per liter) and maintained at that concentration for 40
      minutes. Plasma free insulin, epinephrine, norepinephrine, cortisol,
      and growth hormone were measured frequently during each study. Sleep
      was monitored by polysomnography. RESULTS: The plasma glucose and free
      insulin concentrations were similar in both groups during all studies.
      During the studies when the subjects were asleep, no one was awakened
      during the hypoglycemic phase, but during the final 30 minutes of the
      studies when the subjects were awake both the patients with diabetes
      and the normal subjects had symptoms of hypoglycemia. In the patients
      with diabetes, plasma epinephrine responses to hypoglycemia were
      blunted when they were asleep (mean [+/-SE] peak plasma epinephrine
      concentration, 70+/-14 pg per milliliter [382+/-76 pmol per liter];
      P=0.3 for the comparison with base line), as compared with when they
      were awake during the day or night (238+/-39 pg per milliliter [1299+/-
      213 pmol per liter] P=0.004 for the comparison with base line, and
      296+/-60 pg per milliliter [1616+/-327 pmol per liter], P=0.004,
      respectively). The patients' plasma norepinephrine responses were also
      reduced during sleep, whereas their plasma cortisol concentrations did
      not increase and their plasma growth hormone concentrations increased
      slightly. The patterns of counterregulatory-hormone responses in the
      normal subjects were similar. CONCLUSIONS: Sleep impairs
      counterregulatory-hormone responses to hypoglycemia in patients with
      diabetes and normal subjects.
AD  - Department of Diabetes and Endocrinology, Princess Margaret Hospital
      for Children, Perth, WA, Australia.
PMID- 0009614256
SO  - N Engl J Med 1998 Jun 4;338(23):1657-62
```

MEDLINE report (continued)

3

GETTING STARTED

PubMed Basic Search

> *http://www.ncbi.nlm.nih.gov/PubMed*

PubMed Advanced Search

> *http://www.ncbi.nlm.nih.gov/PubMed/medline.html*

Chapters 3, 4, and 5 give a brief tour of the major areas of PubMed. Chapter 6 has step-by-step instructions for using the various areas. Chapter 7 has general strategies for conducting searches.

OVERVIEW OF PUBMED SCREENS

On the Basic and Advanced Search pages you see the following gray sidebar, with links to other areas of PubMed:

Help
Extensive document which is available from the question mark on the top of every PubMed screen.

Advanced Search
Search screen where you can specify which field to search and modify your search afterward.

Journal Browser
Search screen to find journal titles using a whole word or part of a word.

Citation Matcher
Search screen to find an article by journal, date, volume, and/or page. Can be used to generate a table of contents for an issue, or bibliographic references for a paper.

Overview

Help

New/Noteworthy
NEW June 10, 1998

Clinical Alerts

Advanced Search

Clinical Queries

Journal Browser   NEW

MeSH Browser

Citation Matcher

Loansome Doc

Internet Grateful Med

Clinical Alerts
Reports on clinical studies of special importance.

Clinical Queries
A basic search with pre-set algorithms for results related to therapy, diagnosis, etiology, or prognosis.

MeSH Browser
Search screen to find a term in the Medical Subject Headings, read a definition, see where it is located in the hierarchy of MeSH concepts, choose subheadings for a term, and start a search on the term.

HELP

The Help screen for PubMed is a single Web page with links to various topics. It is a basic guide to PubMed, and includes screen captures, descriptions of the search fields, lists of subheadings, and other information.

PubMed Help

(Last Updated: April 1998)

Database Coverage (MEDLINE, PREMEDLINE, & Publisher Supplied citations)

Basic Mode
Subject Searching
    Author Names
    Journal Titles
    Automatic Term Mapping
        MeSH Translation Table
        Journals Translation Table
    Truncation
    Phrase Searching
    Number of documents to display per page
    Entrez Date limit
Advanced Search Mode
    Search Fields
    Search Modes
    Automatic Mode
    List Terms Mode
    Add Term(s) to Query
    Modify Current Query
    Current Query - Retrieving Documents
MeSH Browser
Document Summary Page (Search Results)
    Details Button
    Displaying Documents
        Display Formats
    Printing and Saving
    See Related Articles Link

PubMed Help

CLINICAL ALERTS

A Clinical Alert is a notice of preliminary results from a research study. These are released because it is felt that the findings are pointing strongly in one direction. Waiting until the end of the study to publish the results (and thus make use of the research) would needlessly increase the chance for illness or death in some patients. Clinical Alerts are published by the NIH, and began in 1991; there are 17 alerts at this time, the latest having to do with red blood cell transfusions in children with sickle cell anemia. They are listed in chronological order, with the most recent first. A clinical alert typically explains the study and current findings and gives contact information for the principal investigators.

There are currently 17 clinical alerts:

Periodic Transfusions Lower Stroke Risk in Children with Sickle Cell Anemia
      National Heart, Lung, and Blood Institute (NHLBI)
      September 18, 1997

Adjuvant Therapy of Breast Cancer - Tamoxifen Update.
      National Cancer Institute (NCI)
      November 30, 1995

To Ophthalmologists -- Findings from the Endophthalmitis Vitrectomy Study (EVS).
      National Eye Institute (NEI)
      October 13, 1995

Bypass Over Angioplasty for Patients With Diabetes.
      National Heart, Lung, and Blood Institute (NHLBI)
      September 21, 1995

Drug Treatment for Sickle Cell Anemia Announced January 30, 1995.
      National Heart, Lung, and Blood Institute (NHLBI)
      January 30, 1995

National Eye Institute Announces Ischemic Optic Neuropathy Decompression Trial (IONDT) Findings.
      National Eye Institute (NEI)
      January 3, 1995

Clinical Alerts

BASIC SEARCH

- Go to the PubMed **Basic Search** page
  http://www.ncbi.nlm.nih.gov/PubMed.
- Click to position the cursor into the text box beneath the
  Search button, then type the word or words you are searching for. The best strategy is to type multiple terms which
  describe the topic. For example:

    thalassemia major transfusion therapy
    septic arthritis prevention ciprofloxacin
    genetic screening tay-sachs

  PubMed will combine multiple words using Boolean AND. It
  will also connect phrases intelligently (putting *septic* with
  arthritis into one phrase, and *genetic* with *screening*.) To
  search for an **author**, type the **last name first, followed by
  initial(s)**.

  For example: *brown jb* You can also use one initial: *brown j*

- Click **Search** or press the **Enter** key.

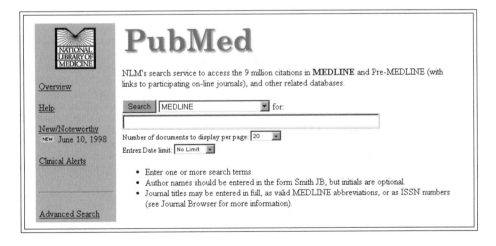

PubMed basic search

DOCUMENT LIST

The document list is displayed after a search. This shows the results, 20 to a page, arranged in reverse chronological order (i.e., most recent first) according to the date the citations were added to PubMed. Information on each article includes author, title of the article, title of the journal, volume, issue, page, and MEDLINE (UI) and PubMed (PMID) numerical identifiers.

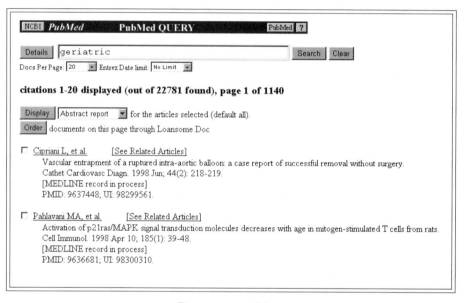

Document List

- Use the text box at the top to do a new search or click PubMed in the titlebar at the top.
- Click **Clear** to clear the field for a new word.

- Click the **Go To** button at the bottom to see the next page of results.

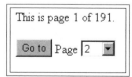

DISPLAY ABSTRACTS

- Click on the author's name to see the abstract (if available) for an article. See Chapter 2 for a explanation of an abstract and its form in MEDLINE.

> ☐ Lambert C, et al.   [See Related Articles]
> Pancreatic cancer as a second tumour following treatment of Hodgkin's disease.
> Br J Radiol. 1998 Feb; 71(842): 229-232.
> PMID: 9579190; UI: 98240353.

Click author name to display abstract

- The default type of report generated is the **Abstract Report**, shown below.

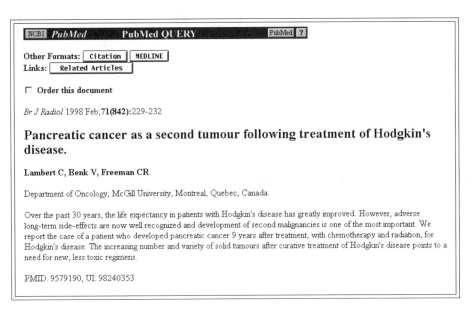

Abstract Report

- Click **Display** to see the **Abstract Report** for all the citations displayed on a page. To see abstracts for selected articles, place a check in the box by each of them, then click **Display**.

☐ Gress TM, et al.   [See Related Articles]
    [Diagnosis of a "hereditary pancreatitis" by the detection of a mutation in the cationic trypsinogen gene].
    Dtsch Med Wochenschr. 1998 Apr 9; 123(15): 453-456. German.
    PMID: 9581160; UI: 98242261.

☐ Zojer N, et al.   [See Related Articles]
    Chromosomal imbalances in primary and metastatic pancreatic carcinoma as detected by interphase cytogenetics: basic
    findings and clinical aspects.
    Br J Cancer. 1998 Apr; 77(8): 1337-1342.
    PMID: 9579843; UI: 98239446.

☐ Lambert C, et al.   [See Related Articles]
    Pancreatic cancer as a second tumour following treatment of Hodgkin's disease.
    Br J Radiol. 1998 Feb; 71(842): 229-232.
    PMID: 9579190; UI: 98240353.

☐ Ouyang H, et al.   [See Related Articles]
    The BAX gene, the promoter of apoptosis, is mutated in genetically unstable cancers of the colorectum, stomach, and
    endometrium.
    Clin Cancer Res. 1998 Apr; 4(4): 1071-1074.
    PMID: 9563904; UI: 98223393.

Check boxes for display

Use the **Citation Report** to display not only the abstract, but also MeSH terms, substance names, personal name as subject, and grant members that are linked to an article. Note that MeSH major topics are shown with an asterisk.

Br J Radiol 1998 Feb;**71(842):**229-232

Pancreatic cancer as a second tumour following treatment of Hodgkin's disease.

Lambert C, Benk V, Freeman CR

Department of Oncology, McGill University, Montreal, Quebec, Canada.

Over the past 30 years, the life expectancy in patients with Hodgkin's disease has greatly improved. However, adverse long-term side-effects are now well recognized and development of second malignancies is one of the most important. We report the case of a patient who developed pancreatic cancer 9 years after treatment, with chemotherapy and radiation, for Hodgkin's disease. The increasing number and variety of solid tumours after curative treatment of Hodgkin's disease points to a need for new, less toxic regimens.

MeSH Terms:

- Adult
- Case Report
- Follow-Up Studies
- Hodgkin Disease/therapy*
- Human
- Male
- Neoplasms, Radiation-Induced/radiography
- Neoplasms, Radiation-Induced/etiology
- Neoplasms, Second Primary/radiography
- Neoplasms, Second Primary/etiology*
- Pancreatic Neoplasms/radiography
- Pancreatic Neoplasms/etiology*
- Tomography, X-Ray Computed

PMID: 9579190, UI: 98240353

Citation Report

- Use the **MEDLINE Report** for downloading data to biblio-graphic software. This report shows all of the fields and values for the citation. See Appendix D for a list of the two-letter qualifiers and what they designate.
- Select the **Text** option at the bottom when saving for this purpose.

MEDLINE Report

SEE RELATED ARTICLES

This function enables you to perform an instant literature search. (See Chapter 8 for a detailed explanation of the algorithm be-hind this function.) You do not need to know either medical vocabulary or search syntax to run a search using See Related Articles.

- Click the **See Related Articles** link next to any article.
- To choose several articles, click in the check box next to each, then use the **Display** drop-down list and choose **Related Articles**.

The result will be another Document List. **When you run a search using See Related Articles, the document list is shown in order of relevance to the original, *not* in chronological order.** This is important to understand when viewing the document list.

PRINT

- To print the Document List, select a number from the drop-down menu next to **Docs per page**, then click the **Search** button again.

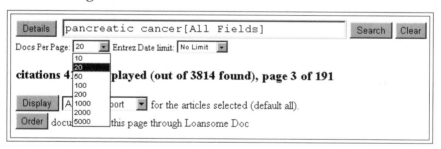

- When the documents are displayed, use the File, Print menu of your browser program.
- To print abstracts, display the abstracts as explained earlier in this chapter, then use the File, Print menu of your browser program.

SAVE RESULTS TO A FILE

To save the Document List screen, use the File, Save menu of your Web browser.

To save a report, first display the report, then scroll to the bottom of the screen.

- Select your type of computer (PC, Macintosh, Unix) and type of format (text, HTML). Use HTML only if you want to see the results in a Web browser.

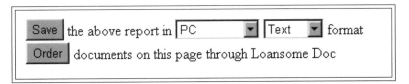

Save report to a file

4 ADVANCED SEARCH

Don't let the phrase *Advanced Search* put you off; using this part of PubMed is not at all difficult. It is *advanced* only in the sense that it has more options than simply typing a word into the Basic Search box. The concepts and functions of these areas are quite easy to grasp. Although you can start the same way as with a Basic Search (by typing a few words), you can also choose which fields to search, or use the List Terms function to show the possibilities for fields such as Publication Types. The choices in Advanced Search are necessary to learn in order to narrow a search to very specific topics or to modify a search.

Before working through this area, you need to understand the way in which information is searchable in a database such as MEDLINE. Boolean logic, as it is called, will come in handy in many databases and programs outside of MEDLINE as well.

BOOLEAN LOGIC

Boolean logic (also called symbolic logic or Boolean algebra) describes the fundamental way to search any database. Whether you will be searching MEDLINE, the Internet, or a staff directory, Boolean logic will be used. It is a fundamental set of concepts which everyone who uses computers should know.

In a database, each separate "thing" that it keeps track of, such as a book, has its own record. For every record there are several categories, called fields. A database can have multiple categories, such as title, author, date of publication, journal, number of pages, type of publication, and so on. The basic way of visualizing a database is as a table:

Title	Author	Date	Journal	Pages
Lop-ear Cats	Jones, DB	11/97	Small Animal	24-36
Barking Dogs	Smith, MB	10/96	Small Animal	57-62
Chirpy Birds	Jones, DB	5/95	Small Animal	10-23

Here we have three imaginary entries in a bibliographic database. All three entries are from the same journal, *Small Animal*.

When information about a collection of items is placed in a database, the database can then be searched in very complex ways. Basically, each field can be searched, or a detailed search can be created from several fields. You can search for all authors named *Smith* or look for books with *cancer* in the title published in the last five years. This allows very precise searching.

Strictly speaking, these concepts describe relationships between elements in the database. There are three concepts to understand: *AND*, *OR*, and *NOT* (sometimes written as *BUT NOT*). The most important is *AND*.

BOOLEAN *AND*

The term *AND* means that both terms or conditions must be present. *AND* limits or narrows a search.

You probably don't want *all* the articles from a given year, only those that deal with bronchodilators, for example. By creating a search which asks for *1997 AND bronchodilators* you limit or restrict the search to citations which must be published in 1997 and on the subject of bronchodilators.

Use AND to reduce the results of a search to a more manageable number. One of the secrets of PubMed is that **when you enter a few general terms into the Basic or Advanced search box, PubMed automatically creates a Boolean search linking all of the terms with AND.** For example, by searching for *rehydration therapy cholera 1997*, PubMed actually searches for *rehydration therapy AND cholera AND 1997*.

To review:

AND   = *both* must be present   =   limiting (intersection)

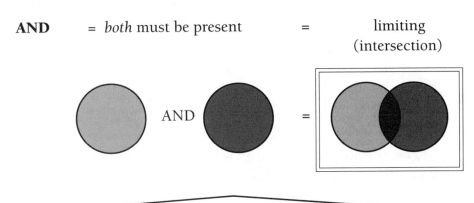

BOOLEAN *OR*

The term *OR* means that either term or condition can be present. *OR* expands or widens a search.

Suppose you are searching for the word *hemothorax*, and you want to ensure that British spellings are included. Searching for *hemothorax OR haemothorax* gives you citations that include either one term or the other. If you think of the results of a search as a set, then OR gives you everything that is in either set.

To review:

OR = *either* one or another   =   expanding (union)

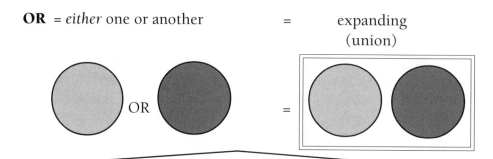

BOOLEAN *NOT*

> The term *NOT* means that one term must be present and the second must *not* be present. *NOT* limits a search by excluding a specific set of items.

The third connector takes the results from an AND search and removes them from consideration. For example, *malabsorption BUT NOT crohn disease* will give citations for all articles dealing with malabsorption, but exclude those which concern Crohn's Disease.

COMPLEX QUESTIONS

The above discussion is limited to pairs of terms, but more complex queries using two or more connectors can be created using AND, OR, and NOT. For example, take a look at the question *(dysphagia AND pneumonia) OR aspiration,* and note the parentheses. This question will give all articles related to aspiration, as well as all articles which are related to dysphagia AND pneumonia.

Click the **Advanced Search** link from the main PubMed screen, or go to ***http://www.ncbi.nlm.nih.gov/PubMed/medline.html***

ENTER MULTIPLE TERMS
INTO AN ADVANCED SEARCH

Remember, the best initial strategy is to enter multiple, general terms. After entering several terms using the Advanced Search screen, you can modify your search by excluding one or more of the terms.

PubMed will apply a detailed search process (see Chapter 8 for an explanation) and link the resultant terms together using Boolean AND and OR. The screen below shows a question, using the terms degenerative arthritis treatment.

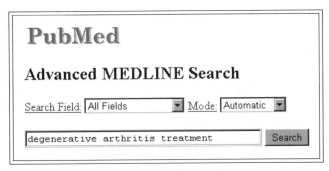

Advanced search

- You may also choose a **Search Field** (e.g. MeSH Terms). For a description of searchable fields in PubMed, see Appendix D or click the underlined **Search Field** link.

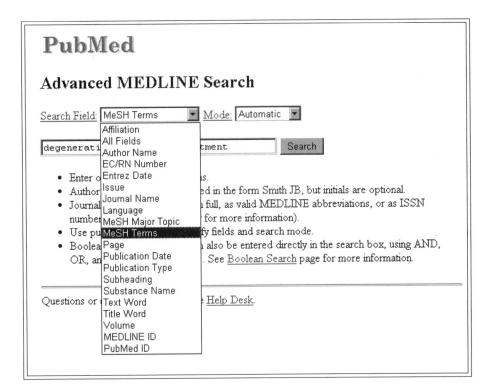

Search Fields in PubMed

CURRENT QUERY

The next screen is the **Current Query**.

At this point you have several choices. You can:

- click **Retrieve ___ Documents** to see a list of the citations
- use the **Add Terms to Query** section to modify your search with more words
- use the **Modify Current Query** section to select specific words from your earlier query or change the Boolean connector between them
- click **Details** to see the syntax and MeSH terms that have been applied to your current search

We will look at each of these in turn.

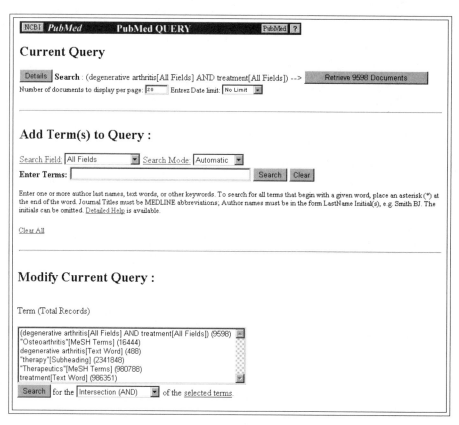

Current Query screen

- Click **Retrieve ___ Documents** button to see the document list.
- To limit your results to the most recent, choose a time period from the **Entrez date limit** box, then click **Retrieve ___ Documents**.

ADD TERM(S) TO QUERY

- Select a Search Field and add a term as you did in the Advanced Search screen.
- Your term is added to the previous query with Boolean AND.

Add Term(s) to Query :

Search Field: `All Fields ▼`   Search Mode: `Automatic ▼`

Enter Terms: `prosthesis`   `Search`   `Clear`

Add terms to query

MODIFY CURRENT QUERY

Use this to add Boolean AND, OR, BUT NOT to two or more terms.

- Hold down the Ctrl key and click on one or more terms.
- Select the Boolean connector to use between the terms.
- Click **Search**.

Modify Current Query :

Term (Total Records)

```
(degenerative arthritis[All Fields] AND treatment[All Fields]) (9598)
"Osteoarthritis"[MeSH Terms] (16444)
degenerative arthritis[Text Word] (488)
"therapy"[Subheading] (2341848)
"Therapeutics"[MeSH Terms] (980788)
treatment[Text Word] (986351)
prosthesis[All Fields] (158365)
```

`Search` for the `Intersection (AND)` of the selected terms.

```
Intersection (AND)
Union (OR)
Difference (BUTNOT)
Range
```

Questions or com   Desk.

Modify Current Query

Note that PubMed keeps track of each query.

Hold down the Ctrl key to select multiple terms to add to a query.

The word *Intersection* is a synonym for Boolean AND.

The word *Union* is a synonym for Boolean OR.

DETAILS (OF YOUR SEARCH)

PubMed automatically looks to see if there is a synonymous MeSH term for the word(s) you enter. (See Chapter 8 for more information.) You can use the Details button of the **Current Query** or **Document List** screen at any time to see the exact logic and terms which PubMed is using for your search.

The **Details** button on the Document List screen shows that PubMed is able to translate the individual words (*total* and *hip*) correctly when a search is done for the phrase *total hip replacement*.

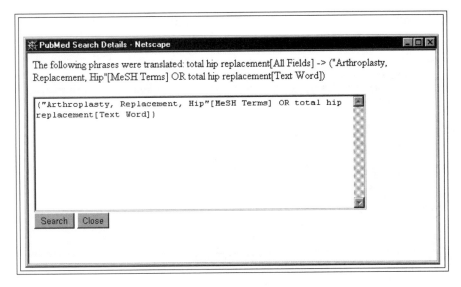

Details of a search

The Details function uses JavaScript (a computer programming language), so you must be using a Web browser which can read JavaScript. If you are using Netscape Navigator version 2.0 or higher, or Internet Explorer version 3.0 or higher, you should not have any problem.

Details can often be used to see what MeSH terms PubMed has translated your search words into, or to modify the search.

LIST TERMS

This function is located next to the Search Field in any of the Advanced Search screens. Rather than running a search automatically, List Terms allows you to choose from a list of possible terms. You choose a search field, search for a term in the resulting list, then add that term to a query. It is most useful with MeSH terms, subheadings, and publication types. You can use List Terms to find exact medical terminology, if you are unfamiliar with a specific vocabulary. (Or you can use the MeSH Browser).

List Terms is available from any of the **Advanced Search** screens.

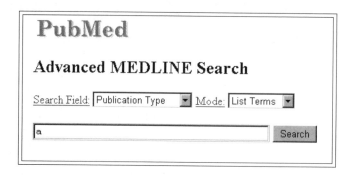

List terms

- Select a field to search, such as Publication Type.
- For **Mode**, select **List Terms**.

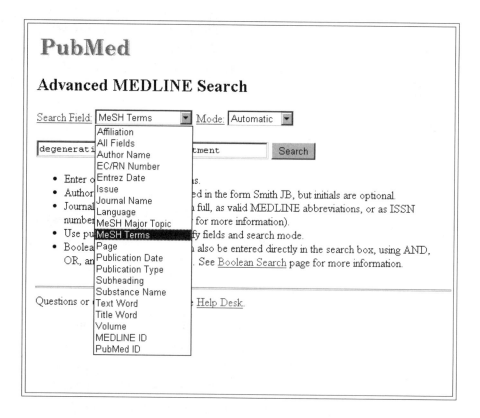

Searchable fields in PubMed

You then see a screen with terms. Below are the possible terms for **Publication Type**. The list here is limited, whereas some other fields (MeSH terms, text word) have lists which run into the thousands.

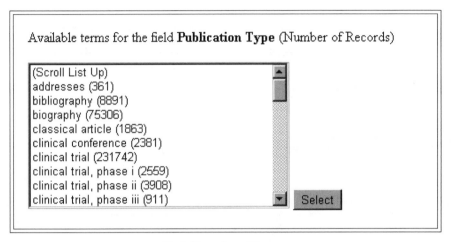

Available terms for the field **Publication Type** (Number of Records)

(Scroll List Up)
addresses (361)
bibliography (8891)
biography (75306)
classical article (1863)
clinical conference (2381)
clinical trial (231742)
clinical trial, phase i (2559)
clinical trial, phase ii (3908)
clinical trial, phase iii (911)

Select

Publication Types

PUBLICATION TYPES

Publication types can be used to narrow a search, by limiting it to one or more types of information. A publication type is a kind of document such as review article, clinical trial, letter to the editor, historical article, practice guideline, review of the literature, or interview. Others are clinical trial (phase i, ii, iii, iv), meeting report, consensus development conference, or legal brief. See Appendix D for a complete list of publication types.

There are several types of *review*, which serve different purposes:

Review   all types of review shown below
Review, academic   comprehensive, critical, or analytical review
Review, multicase   review with epidemiological applications
Review of reported cases review of known cases of a disease

Review literature   general review article
Review tutorial   broad review for the non-specialist
                           or student
Scientific Integrity Review reports from the U.S. Office of
                           Scientific Integrity

Note that the *Review, academic* will be especially useful for the
professional, whereas the *Review tutorial* will be useful for students and others who are not familiar with the subject.

To display and select a publication type, use the **List Mode** in
the Advanced Search. Click **All Fields**, select **Publication
Types**, type the letter "a" and click **Search**.

CLINICAL QUERIES

A Clinical Query is similar to a basic search in that you have a
single text box to enter your search word(s). A Clinical Query,
however, performs a pre-formatted Boolean search, using specific
filters on your subject. There are four choices: therapy, diagnosis, etiology, or prognosis. For any of these you can choose to
have an emphasis on sensitivity or on specificity. The results are
shown as a Document List. See Chapter 8 for more information
about the exact words that a Clinical Query uses to conduct its
search.

- Choose a category (therapy, diagnosis, etiology, prognosis).

- Choose an emphasis:

    1. higher **sensitivity** gives a wider search (increases true
       positive results).
    2. higher **specificity** narrows the search, giving more rel-
       evant results (decreases true negative results).

PubMed

Clinical Queries using Research Methodology Filters

This specialized search is intended for clinicians and has built-in search "filters" based largely upon Haynes RB et al.. Four study categories--therapy, diagnosis, etiology, prognosis--are provided, and you may indicate whether you wish your search to be more sensitive (i.e., include most relevant articles but probably including some less relevant ones) or more specific (i.e. including mostly relevant articles but probably omit a few). See this table for details regarding filtering.

Indicate the category and emphasis below:
Category: ⦿ therapy ○ diagnosis ○ etiology ○ prognosis
Emphasis: ○ sensitivity ⦿ specificity

Enter subject search (do not repeat any of the words above):

| keratosis | Search |

Reset

Clinical Queries

To give an example of the automatic syntax that PubMed creates when you run a Clinical Query, here is the query generated when you type *marfan* and choose *prognosis* and *sensitivity*:

(marfan AND

((sensitivity and specificity) OR sensitivity) OR

((diagnosis OR diagnostic use) OR specificity)))

Even the above is simplified, because PubMed also looks in particular fields (MeSH terms or subheadings) for each of these words. The complete search as shown by PubMed is:

(marfan[All Fields] AND

(("Sensitivity and Specificity"[MeSH Terms] OR sensitivity[WORD]) OR

(("diagnosis"[Subheading] OR "diagnostic use"[Subheading]) OR

specificity[WORD])))

What you see above is the question, or query, which PubMed sends to the database. If we were to ask the question in common language, it might look like this:

1.   Look for the word *marfan* in all the different fields of
      MEDLINE (title word, abstract, MeSH, etc.).

2.   Take the set of results from #1 and look for the MeSH
      terms *sensitivity and specificity* or the word *sensitivity*.

3.   Take the set of results from #1 and look for the subhead-
      ing *diagnosis* or the subheading *diagnostic use*.

4.   Take the set of results from #1 and look for the word
      specificity.

5.   Display all the results from #2-4.

Numbers 2-4 show how AND is used to limit a search (*marfan*) to
certain aspects. Number 5 shows how the term OR combines all the
results of all these AND searches into one final set.

This chapter covered quite a bit: Boolean logic, search fields,
listing terms, adding terms to a query or modifying it, publication types, and clinical queries. If you have made it this far, the
end is in sight! The next chapter finishes this overview of
PubMed functions by reviewing the MeSH and Journal browsers.

5

MESH AND JOURNAL BROWSERS

MESH: MEDICAL SUBJECT HEADINGS

MeSH is a thesaurus and hierarchy of concepts. Below is an example of the how the MeSH browser displays the structure, in this case the point for *cerebrovascular disorders*.

```
Top of MeSH Tree
    Nervous System Diseases
        Central Nervous System Diseases
        Brain Diseases
        Cerebrovascular Disorders
            Carotid Artery Diseases
                Carotid Artery Thrombosis
                Carotid Stenosis
                Moyamoya Disease

            Cerebral Amyloid Angiopathy
            Cerebral Aneurysm
            Cerebral Anoxia
            Cerebral Arteriosclerosis
            Cerebral Arteriovenous Malformations
            Cerebral Artery Diseases
            Cerebral Embolism and Thrombosis
                Carotid Artery Thrombosis
                Sinus Thrombosis
                Wallenberg's Syndrome

            Cerebral Hemorrhage
                Hematoma, Epidural
                Hematoma, Subdural
                Subarachnoid Hemorrhage
```

Example of MeSH hierarchy

Most terms in MeSH have a broader conceptual level, or parent, which they fall under, as well as more specific terms, or child concepts, beneath them. (The child/parent metaphor comes from looking at a family "tree," where children are listed beneath their parents.) Beneath *tetanus* is the term *bacillaceae infections,* and beneath *bacillaceae infections* is *Clostridium infections.* It is important to understand that a term has more narrow or precise headings beneath it, because a PubMed search automatically includes or "explodes" these subcategories. For some searches you may want to turn off this automatic explosion.

MeSH is arguably the most important aspect of MEDLINE. Once an article is selected for inclusion in MEDLINE, a staff member from the National Library of Medicine assigns a dozen or more terms from the MeSH vocabulary of 18,000 terms and phrases. MeSH is both a thesaurus - a collection of words and synonyms - and a hierarchical system of concepts, similar to a table of contents. Each term in MeSH includes a definition.

MeSH is updated each year; new terms are added as they come into use, and older ones are deleted as they become obsolete. (In PubMed, however, you can often use an outdated term and it will translate into the current term. A search on *grippe* automatically translates to the MeSH term *influenza,* and *dropsy* translates to *edema.*)

Appendix D has more details about MeSH, including listings of the subheadings, age groups, subheadings for pharmaceuticals, searchable fields, publication types, and two-letter category qualifiers.

You can see the MeSH terms assigned to an article by viewing the Citation report or the MEDLINE report.

MESH BROWSER

The MeSH browser allows you to choose MeSH terms, read definitions, restrict your query to subheadings of that term, and apply them to a search. It is especially useful for terminologies or subject areas with which you are unfamiliar.

One advantage to using MeSH is that a search on a term automatically includes the terms beneath it; in other words, the
parent term is expanded to include the *child* terms (or branches
of the tree hierarchy) beneath it. This makes your search more
comprehensive. When using the MeSH browser you can also
choose *not* to have a term or terms exploded, thereby making the
search more narrow.

There is no single way to navigate through the MeSH browser.
Different screens will appear depending on whether your term is
an exact match for a MeSH word; can't be found; or appears in
multiple places in the MeSH hierarchy.

- From the starting PubMed screen click the **MeSH Browser**
  link in the gray sidebar.
- Type your word into the text box and click **Browse**.

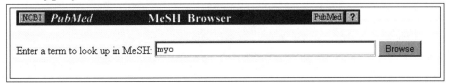

MeSH browser

- If your term does not have an exact match, PubMed will
  display a list of possibilities, as below.
- Select a term and click **Browse This Item**.

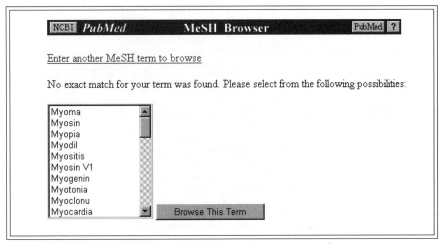

MeSH browser – no exact match

MESH TERM SCREEN

You now see the term with its definition. In the MeSH tree hierarchy your term appears in bold. Above it are higher levels in the MeSH conceptual hierarchy, and beneath it are terms which fall within the area of your concept. All the other terms are linked to their corresponding points in the hierarchy. You can jump to those levels by clicking on a term.

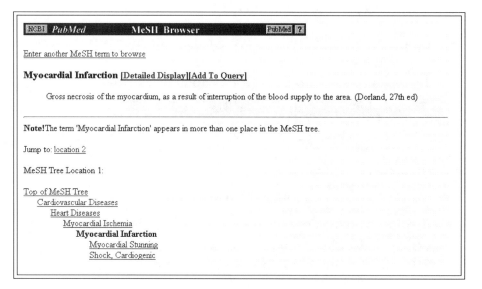

MeSH simple display with Tree Hierarchy

At this point you have several choices. You can:

- click any of the items in the MeSH tree to see a different level of the MeSH hierarchy
- click **Detailed Display** if you wish to see subheadings for this term
- click **Add to Query**, then **Return to PubMed** to run a search on this term
- click **Enter another MeSH term to browse** if you wish to look up another term

We will look at each of these in turn.

- Click **Heart Diseases** to see the screen below.

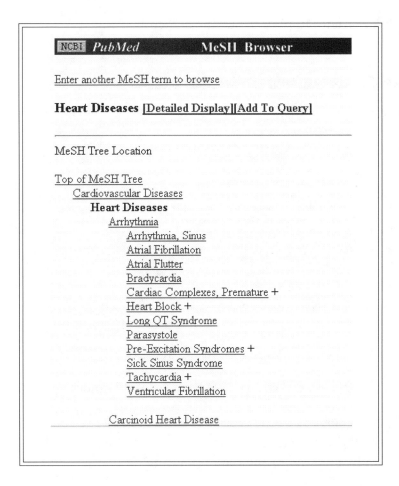

Another level in the MeSH tree

DETAILED DISPLAY

Click **Detailed Display** to see the screen below.

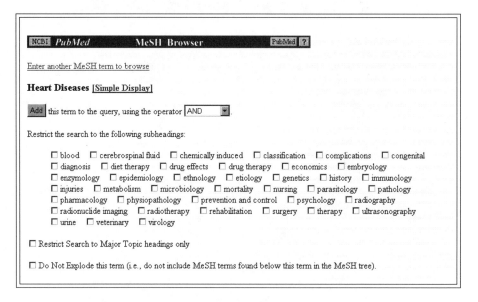

MeSH detailed display

From the **Detailed Display** you have several choices. You can:

- add the term to your query
- restrict the search to one or more subheadings of a MeSH term by clicking in the corresponding box, and then add it to the query
- restrict your search to **Major Topic** headings, and then add it to the query
- choose **Do Not Explode this term** to keep the search more narrow and focused, and then add it to the query. Remember that MeSH terms and subheadings are automatically exploded, which means that terms found beneath them in the MeSH hierarchy are included.

We will simply add the term to the query for now.

- Click **Add To Query**.
- Then click **Return to PubMed** to run a search on this term.

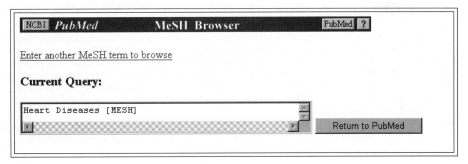

Add to query

BROWSE FROM THE TOP OF THE TREE

When you browse the tree itself, you look at the hierarchy and expand a branch until you come to the term. (This is similar to the process of expanding the folders or directories in a Windows-based computer.) The list displayed is actually the second level of the MeSH hierarchy. See Appendix D for a list of the top-level MeSH hierarchy.

- Click the word **PubMed** at the top of the screen to return to the starting screen.
- Scroll down to click the **MeSH Browser**.
- Click **Start at the top of the tree**.

Top of the MeSH tree hierarchy

- A plus sign (+) indicates that the term has sub-levels.

- Click on any term with a plus sign to see the levels below it, such as **Bacterial Infections and Mycoses**.

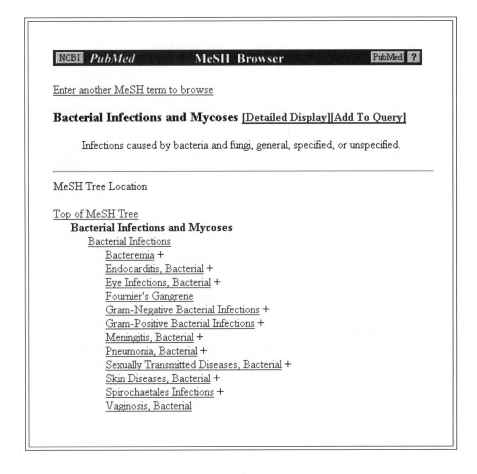

Sublevel in the MeSH tree hierarchy

At this point you have the same choices as noted above. You can:

- click any of the items in the MeSH tree to see a different level of the MeSH hierarchy

- click **Detailed Display** if you wish to see subheadings for this term

- click **Add to Query**, then **Return to PubMed** to run a search on this term

- click **Enter another MeSH term to browse** if you wish to look up another term

JOURNAL BROWSER

This function allows you to search for a journal by name, ISSN, or MEDLINE abbreviation. Once you find a journal, you can run a search on articles from it, or return to the Advanced Search page to limit a complex search to that journal. To search for part of a word, use the asterisk truncation symbol (*), for example `psyc*`

- Click the **Journal Browser** link in the gray sidebar to start.
- Type a complete word such as `psychology`.

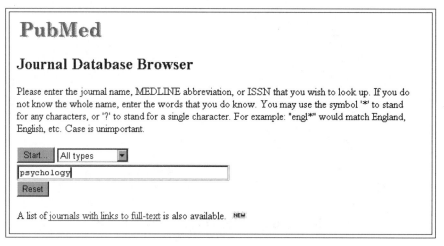

Journal Browser

- Click the abbreviated name of a journal on the right to run a search on all articles from that journal, or
- Click **Next matches** below the list to see the next group of journals.

```
 ┌──────┐                                        ┌────────┬───┐
 │ NCBI │       Journal Database Browser         │ Entrez │ ? │
 └──────┘                                        └────────┴───┘
```

Found 56 journal(s)

Title	ISSN	Medline abbr.
AMERICAN JOURNAL OF COMMUNITY PSYCHOLOGY	0091-0562	Am J Community Psychol
AMERICAN JOURNAL OF PSYCHOLOGY	0002-9556	Am J Psychol
ANNUAL REVIEW OF PSYCHOLOGY	0066-4308	Annu Rev Psychol
BIOLOGICAL PSYCHOLOGY	0301-0511	Biol Psychol
PSYCHOLOGY AND AGING	0882-7974	Psychol Aging
BRITISH JOURNAL OF EDUCATIONAL PSYCHOLOGY	0007-0998	Br J Educ Psychol
BRITISH JOURNAL OF MATHEMATICAL AND STATISTICAL PSYCHOLOGY	0007-1102	Br J Math Stat Psychol
BRITISH JOURNAL OF MEDICAL PSYCHOLOGY	0007-1129	Br J Med Psychol
BRITISH JOURNAL OF PSYCHOLOGY	0007-1269	Br J Psychol
BRITISH JOURNAL OF SOCIAL PSYCHOLOGY	0144-6665	Br J Soc Psychol

Next matches

Results of journal search

CITATION MATCHER

The **Citation Matcher** is a specialized function, useful for publishers and others who need to do very targeted searches using Volume, Issue, or Author information. It can also be used to generate accurate references for a bibliography, thereby avoiding the time and errors involved in typing such references manually. Probably its most useful function for the general professional is the ability to generate a table of contents for a specific journal.

First find the title of the journal, for example, *Investigational New Drugs,* using the **Journal Browser** as explained above. Enter the year and month of the issue, in any of the following formats:

1998
1998/04
1998/04/15

PubMed

Citation Matcher for Single Articles

Enter information about the article you wish to find.

Journal: `canadian family physician`

Date: `1997/11`

Volume: `_____` Issue: `_____` First page: `_____`

Author's last name and initials (e.g., Smith BJ) `_____`

`Search` `Clear`

Citation matcher

The result will be a Document List screen listing the articles from that issue.

6

EXERCISES FOR LEARNING PUBMED

INTRODUCTION

Use this chapter to practice searching PubMed. Working through the first seven exercises will give you basic skills in using PubMed, especially the **extremely important technique of entering multiple terms.**

If you learn to use computers easily, skip this chapter and concentrate on chapters 3-5. However, if you need guided practice, these exercises will acquaint you with most of the PubMed functions. To make each exercise independent, most exercises end by returning to the PubMed Basic Search screen.

List of Exercises

BASIC SEARCH (p. 61)

- Basic search - multiple terms
- Basic search - expand acronym
- Start a new search from the document list screen
- Limit a search to recent articles
- Change the number of articles to display
- Display selected abstracts
- Save abstracts to a text file
Time Out: Practice

ADVANCED SEARCH (p. 64)

- Add terms to an advanced search
- Modify current query
- Search for a MeSH major topic
Time Out: Practice

ADVANCED SEARCH CONTINUED (p. 65)

- See related articles
- List terms – all fields
- List terms – publication types
- List terms – substance name
Time Out: Practice

MESH BROWSER (p. 67)

- MeSH browser
- MeSH browser – navigate hierarchy
- MeSH browser – translate term
- Clinical query – quick search
Time Out: Practice

JOURNAL BROWSER (p. 69)

- Find a journal name from its abbreviation
- Find a journal from a subject word
- Find a journal from a partial word
- Citation matcher – find a table of contents
- View a full-text article on the Internet
- See a list of all journals with full text
Time Out: Practice

BASIC SEARCH

BASIC SEARCH - MULTIPLE TERMS

Entering multiple terms is the best way to do a quick search in PubMed. Think through your topic, then enter a brief description, as with this exercise.

- Go to the **Basic Search** screen
  http://www.ncbi.nlm.nih.gov/PubMed

- Type `thalassemia major transfusion therapy complications` into the text box and click **Search**.

- Click **Details** and note that PubMed created a complex Boolean statement by connecting each term with AND. Note also that it recognized *major* as belonging in the phrase *thalassemia major* rather than treating it as a separate word.

- Click the browser's **Back** button until you return to the PubMed starting screen, or click the gray PubMed button on the top title bar.

BASIC SEARCH - EXPAND ACRONYM

- From the PubMed starting screen, search for `ptca` (Percutaneous Transluminal Coronary Angioplasty) by typing the abbreviation. You do not have to capitalize.

- Note how many article citations were found.

- Click **Details** to see how PubMed translated the abbreviation into its MeSH equivalent.

- Click **Close** to close the Details box.

- Click the underlined name of the first author to see the abstract report for this citation.

- Click the browser's **Back** button until you return to the PubMed starting screen, or click the gray PubMed button on the top title bar.

START A NEW SEARCH FROM THE DOCUMENT LIST SCREEN

- (continued from previous exercise) Click the **Clear** button at the top of the screen.

- Type gamma globulin into the text box and click **Search** to run a new search.

LIMIT A SEARCH TO RECENT ARTICLES

- (continued from previous exercise) Click the **Clear** button at the top of the screen.

- Click the **Entrez Date Limit** and select 1 year.

- Type ptca in the text box and click **Search**.

- Note that there are fewer articles than in the previous exercise with *ptca*.

- Click the browser's **Back** button until you return to the PubMed starting screen, or click the gray PubMed button on the top title bar.

CHANGE THE NUMBER OF ARTICLES TO DISPLAY

Use this function to allow easier printing of a list of citations. You can display (and print) up to 5,000 citations from one screen.

- From the PubMed starting screen, click **Number of documents to display per page** and select 200.

- Type ptca in the text box and click **Search**.

- Note that the number of references is the same as the original search, but the number of total pages is reduced.

- Scroll to the bottom and use the **Go to** button to see the next batch of citations.

- Click the browser's **Back** button until you return to the PubMed starting screen, or click the gray PubMed button on the top title bar.

DISPLAY SELECTED ABSTRACTS

- From the PubMed starting screen, place a check mark in the boxes for the first three citations.

- Click **Display** to see the Abstract Report for these three.

SAVE ABSTRACTS TO A TEXT FILE

- (continued from previous exercise) Scroll to the bottom of the screen.

- Choose the correct format for your computer (PC, Macintosh, or Unix).

- Select **Text** format and click **Save**.

- Note the name and location of the file.

- Start a word processor on your computer and open the file which contains the abstracts.

- Use the File, Print menu to print a paper copy.

- Close the word processor and return to the browser.

- Click the browser's **Back** button until you return to the PubMed starting screen, or click the gray PubMed button on the top title bar.

TIME OUT: PRACTICE

1. Use a multiple-term search to find articles on *complications* following *surgery* on the *bile duct* for *gallstones*.
2. Use a multi-term search to find if *ciprofloxacin* can be used for *prevention of septic arthritis*.
3. Use a multi-term search to find articles relating *sleep apnea* and *Creutzfeldt-Jakob* disease.
4. Search for articles on *diabetic ketosis* in the last month.
5. Search for articles on *genetic screening* for *Tay-Sachs* disease in the *Ashkenazi* population.

ADVANCED SEARCH

ADD TERMS TO AN ADVANCED SEARCH

- From the PubMed starting screen, click the **Advanced Search** link.

- Search for articles related to bone marrow. Note the number of results.

- In **Add Terms to Query**, enter transplantation and search for it as a **MeSH term.** Note the number of results.

- In **Add Terms to Query**, enter radiation and search for it as a **MeSH term**. Note the number of results.

- In **Add Terms to Query**, enter total-body and search for it in **All Fields**.

MODIFY CURRENT QUERY

- (Continued from previous exercise) Scroll to the bottom of the screen after the previous exercise.

- Note the number of results for each part of your query.

- Select **transplantation**. Hold down the **Ctrl** key and select **radiation**.

- In the text box below the terms, click **Intersection (AND)** and select **Difference (BUTNOT)** instead.

- This searches for the subject transplantation but excludes articles related to radiation.

SEARCH FOR A MESH MAJOR TOPIC

- (Continued from previous exercise) In **Add Terms to Query**, enter monoclonal antibodies and search for it as a **MeSH Major Topic**. This limits the search to articles for which the main focus is monoclonal antibodies.

- Scroll down to the bottom of the page. Note that although your current query is limited to transplantation (and not radiation) and monoclonal antibodies, the previous queries are listed and you can still work with them.

- Click the browser's **Back** button until you return to the PubMed starting screen, or click the gray PubMed button on the top title bar.

TIME OUT: PRACTICE

1. Find an article related to *dehydration-related deaths* and *hyperthermia* by searching for both as MeSH Major Topics.

2. Find recent articles on the efficacy of *doxapram* in the treatment of *neonatal apnea*. (Hint: use the Substance Name field for doxapram.)

3. Compare the number of citations listed in MEDLINE for *epidural anesthesia* under Title Word versus the number listed under MeSH Major Topic. This demonstrates why it is useful to use MeSH terms for the more inclusive categories of a search.

ADVANCED SEARCH (CONTINUED)

SEE RELATED ARTICLES

- From the PubMed Advanced Search screen, search for the PubMed Unique Identifier *9565487*. This is a report in *MMWR* on the outbreak of Rift Valley Fever in Kenya and Somalia in 1997.

- Click **See Related Articles**.

- Scroll down and note how PubMed has accomplished an instant literature search.

- Click the browser's **Back** button until you return to the PubMed starting screen, or click the gray PubMed button on the top title bar.

LIST TERMS – ALL FIELDS

- From the PubMed Advanced Search screen, enter `cachexia` in the text box, and select **List Terms** as the Mode.

- In the **Available terms** box, note the variations that are possible.

- Select one of the variations such as *cachexia/metabolism*, then **Retrieve** the citations.

- Click the browser's **Back** button until you return to the PubMed starting screen, or click the gray PubMed button on the top title bar.

LIST TERMS – PUBLICATION TYPES

- From the PubMed Advanced Search screen, search for `acute abdomen` (**All Fields**).

- In the **Add Term(s) to Query**, select **Publication Type** as the **Search Field** and **List Terms** as the mode.

- Click **Search**.

- The **Available terms** box will show the publication types available.

- Click **guideline,** then click **Select**.

- Retrieve the documents. These will be guidelines for the treatment of acute abdomen. You can use the List Terms feature this way to select a document type for a search.

- Click the browser's **Back** button until you return to the PubMed starting screen, or click the gray PubMed button on the top title bar.

LIST TERMS – SUBSTANCE NAME

- You were told of a report on drinking green tea with a medication that starts with "doxo" but you didn't catch the full name.

- From the PubMed Advanced Search screen, type doxo in the text box, select **Substance Name** as the **Search Field** and **List Terms** as the Mode.

- In the **Available terms** box, click **doxorubicin,** then click **Select**.

- In the **Add terms to Query** box, change the **Search Field** back to **All Fields**, and the **Mode** back to **Automatic**. Type green tea and click **Search**.

- Retrieve your results.

TIME OUT: PRACTICE

At this stage, if you have worked through the preceding exercises, you will be able to do a search in many different ways. There is no single "correct" way to search MEDLINE.

1. Search for adverse effects of *amniocentesis*.

2. Search for *clinical trials* involving *Non-Hodgkin's lymphoma*.

3. Find articles which have the words *concussion* and *sports* in the title.

4. Use the See Related Articles function to do a rapid literature search on immunization for chickenpox.

MESH BROWSER

MESH BROWSER

- From the PubMed starting screen, click on **MeSH Browser.**

- Type kawasaki and click **Browse**.

- Note that PubMed translates *kawasaki* to *Mucocutaneous Lymph Node Syndrome*.

- Choose **Mortality** as a subheading, then click the **Add** button. (Add this term to the query.)

- Click **Return to PubMed** to run the search, then **Retrieve** the results.

- Click the browser's **Back** button until you return to the PubMed starting screen, or click the gray PubMed button on the top title bar.

MESH BROWSER – NAVIGATE HIERARCHY

- From the PubMed starting screen, click on **MeSH Browser.**

- Type hyponatremia and click **Browse**.

- Click **Nutritional and Metabolic Diseases.** Note how you were able to move from a specific condition to a listing of the whole category of metabolic conditions.

- Click the browser's **Back** button until you return to the PubMed starting screen, or click the gray PubMed button on the top title bar.

MESH BROWSER – TRANSLATE TERM

- From the PubMed starting screen, click on **MeSH Browser.**

- Type stroke and click **Browse**.

- Note that PubMed translated the common term to Cerebrovascular Disorders. Scroll down to see a clickable listing of these disorders.

- Click the browser's **Back** button until you return to the PubMed starting screen, or click the gray PubMed button on the top title bar.

CLINICAL QUERY – QUICK SEARCH

- From the PubMed starting screen, click **Clinical Queries**.

- Search for osteomyelitis, using **therapy** as the **Category** and **specificity** (fewer articles) as the **Emphasis**.

- Click **Details** to see the syntax that PubMed actually uses for this search.

- Look through the results to see how useful this mode of searching is. Note that you cannot modify the search through an Add terms box. To modify this kind of search, you will have to work with the Boolean expression in the Details box.

TIME OUT: PRACTICE

1. Use the MeSH Browser to find what the complications are for *Down Syndrome*.

2. Use the MeSH Browser to see what type of organism is *Legionella*.

3. Use the MeSH Browse to get a quick listing of *antibiotics*.

4. Continue the above search. Use the Detailed Display to find *adverse effects* of *Amphotericin B*. On the Current Query screen, use Add Terms to limit the search to *neutropenia* as a MeSH term.

JOURNAL BROWSER

FIND A JOURNAL NAME FROM ITS ABBREVIATION

- From the PubMed starting screen, type congestive heart failure and press **Enter**.

- Find the abbreviated name of the journal immediately below the first article title.

- Highlight this name and select **Edit, Copy**.

- Click on the word **PubMed** in the button bar at the top of the screen to return to the main screen.

- Scroll down and click **Journal Browser**.

- Paste the abbreviation into the text box and click **Start.**

- This gives you the full name and International Standard Serial Number (ISSN) for the journal.

- Click the abbreviated name link to run a search on all articles from that journal.

- Click **Entrez Date Limit** and select **30 days** to see only articles entered in the last month.

- Click the browser's **Back** button until you return to the PubMed starting screen, or click the gray PubMed button on the top title bar.

FIND A JOURNAL FROM A SUBJECT WORD

- From the PubMed starting screen, scroll down and click **Journal Browser**.

- Type nutrition and click **Search**.

- Note that there are 47 journals (at this time) which have the word *nutrition* in the title.

- Click the browser's **Back** button until you return to the PubMed starting screen, or click the gray PubMed button on the top title bar.

FIND A JOURNAL FROM A PARTIAL WORD

- From the PubMed starting screen, scroll down and click **Journal Browser**.

- Type engla* (be sure to include the asterisk) and click **Search**.

- Note that it found the *New England Journal of Medicine*.

- Click the browser's **Back** button until you return to the PubMed starting screen, or click the gray PubMed button on the top title bar.

CITATION MATCHER — FIND A TABLE OF CONTENTS

- From the PubMed starting screen, click **Citation Matcher**

- Type RN for the journal, and 1998/01 for the date. (You can use any of the following formats for date: 1998, 1998/01, 1998/01/15.)

- Click **Search**.

- You will get a list of the articles for *RN* magazine from January 1998.

- Click the browser's **Back** button until you return to the PubMed starting screen, or click the gray PubMed button on the top title bar.

VIEW A FULL-TEXT ARTICLE ON THE INTERNET

- From the PubMed starting screen, scroll down and click **Journal Browser**.

- Type nutrition and click **Search**.

- Select the *Journal of Nutrition* (J.Nutr).

- Click the underlined author's name for an article.

- At the top of the screen, note that to the right of **Links**: is a button for **J. Nutr.**

- Click the **J. Nutr** button to see the full text of that article at the ***http://www.nutrition.org*** site.

- Note that Nutrition.org has provided full backward linking to PubMed, including links to both the original citation and even an automatic Related Articles search. In this way you can visit the Nutrition.org page first, and run an automatic MEDLINE search directly from that page, with one click, without knowing anything about MEDLINE. Click **PubMed Citation** to see your original abstract report using the Nutrition.org linking.

- Click the browser's **Back** button until you return to the PubMed starting screen, or click the gray PubMed button on the top title bar.

SEE A LIST OF ALL JOURNALS WITH FULL TEXT

- From the PubMed starting screen, scroll down and click **Journal Browser**.

- Click the link **journals with links to full-text.**

- Note that there is a link at the top for a file with the complete list of PubMed journals. This file is in zip format, approximately 330 kb.

TIME OUT: PRACTICE

1. Display a list of the last month's articles from the *American Journal of Obstetrics and Gynecology*, using the **Journal Browser** and the **Entrez Date Limit**.

2. Do the same, using the **Citation Matcher**.

3. A friend has sent you an article from the April 1998 issue of *Neurosurgery Clinics of North America*. Knowing that the whole issue is on a single topic, generate a list of articles from that issue.

4. Find the titles of journals that specifically cover heart transplants.

7

STRATEGIES, TIPS, AND TRICKS

STRATEGIES

Searching MEDLINE takes some practice. Simply looking for a broad keyword, such as *hepatitis*, will give too many results to be useful. On the other hand, because MEDLINE is a structured database, you cannot simply enter a question such as "Find me an article on swallowing difficulties with Parkinson's disease" and get helpful results.

Remember that no single strategy will work for every subject – nor is MEDLINE the only source for information. Sometimes you will get better and faster results by calling an expert or by pulling a reference book off the shelf.

DESCRIBE YOUR SUBJECT – SEARCH FOR WHAT YOU WANT

The first thing to do is think about what you are looking for. The mistake many people make when using a database is to enter a single word, such as *cancer*, which gives an overwhelming number of results. Are you interested in the *complications* of pyloric valve surgery, or *infections* relating to the surgery? If you are interested in the use of *broad-spectrum antibiotics*, is it the *contraindications* or *toxicity* which you want? If your overall topic is *influenza*, are you looking for *prevention*, *epidemiology*, *treatment*? The general idea here is to extract the relevant concepts for use in a search.

If you have difficulty doing this, imagine you are trying to describe what you want to a librarian. "I'm looking for..." This may help to clarify your thinking.

Once you know what the exact topic is, the best way to get specific results quickly is to enter the main subjects of your search, such as *epilepsy recurrence surgery* or *neural tube defect surgery complications*. Make sure that words are spelled correctly. (If you don't know how to spell the word, **use a shorter (truncated) form with an asterisk.** See the end of this chapter for instructions about truncation.)

When you type a short phrase describing your topic, such as *cystic fibrosis antibiotic prophylaxis,* PubMed will use its thesaurus to find the correct MeSH term(s), then link them together with the Boolean AND connector. Don't bother with connectives or grammar: just type the main terms or concepts. PubMed often does a very good job with multiple terms. (See the first few exercises in Chapter 6 for examples.) You can use connectives, such as in the phrase *needle biopsy under CT guidance* but PubMed will ignore them anyway.

USE THE MESH BROWSER

You are much more likely to get significant results, and narrow them down quickly, by using the MeSH browser to find your term and any subheadings associated with it. In so doing you will probably re-orient yourself to the overall area you are looking for and discover other concepts or terms that you hadn't considered. This is a good strategy if you don't seem to have a good grasp of what you are looking for, or the scope of your topic.

USE SUBHEADINGS

Become familiar with the subheadings in Appendix D and use
them in a multi-term search. These are the terms which will
often give very specific results, because they are used to further
describe a particular aspect of a MeSH term. As a professional
you use terms such as *toxicity*, *therapy*, or *adverse effects*. By
employing the same terms in a MEDLINE search you greatly
increase the accuracy of your results.

USE LIST TERMS TO GENERATE SUBHEADINGS

Another useful technique is to use the List Terms mode in
Advanced Search to generate a MeSH heading with its associated
subheadings. Use the Advanced Search screen, with MeSH Terms
as the field and List Terms as the mode. For example, simply
entering *seizure* generates the list:

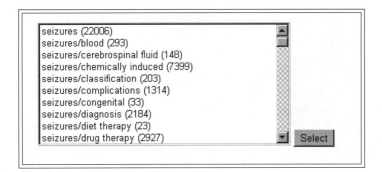

List terms

USE SEE RELATED ARTICLES TO CONDUCT
A QUICK SEARCH

Even if you are relatively uncertain how to proceed in PubMed,
you can run a search on a general term such as *latex allergy*, scan
the articles, and find one that is close to what you need. Then
use See Related Articles to generate a list of citations on your
subject.

TIPS

SEARCH FOR COMMON TERMS IF THAT'S ALL YOU KNOW

Because the MeSH thesaurus is cross-referenced with common terms, you can often do quite well even if you use common terms. For instance, searching for *kidney stone* automatically searches for the MeSH terms *Kidney Calculi*. But this is not always effective. Searching for *blood thinner* does not generate a MeSH term, nor does the phrase *feeding tube*. (However, using the MeSH Browser, *feeding tube* did correctly bring up the phrase *tube, feeding* which links to the MeSH phrase *Enteral Nutrition*)

LEARN AND USE MESH

The MeSH hierarchy and thesaurus is a powerful feature of MEDLINE, and probably the most important aspect for general searches. Because every article is linked to specific MeSH key-words, it is possible to do very precise searches. By using MeSH you are taking advantage of the combined intelligence of the NLM staff who read the articles and assign the terms. The MeSH Browser can enable you to do very rapid searches with a minimum of prior knowledge of MEDLINE or PubMed. It is also a quick way to re-orient yourself to a topic. Finally, the Browser suggests subheadings that you may not have considered, such as etiology, pathology, or instrumentation.

```
Top of MeSH Tree
    Immunologic and Biological Factors
        Immunologic Factors
            Antigens
                Isoantigens
                    Blood Groups
                        ABO Blood-Group System
                        Duffy Blood-Group System
                        I Blood-Group System
                        Kell Blood-Group System
                        Kidd Blood-Group System
                        Lewis Blood-Group System
                            CA-19-9 Antigen

                        Lutheran Blood-Group System
                        MNSs Blood-Group System
                        P Blood-Group System
                        Rh-Hr Blood-Group System
```

Example of MeSH browser listing

MeSH includes links between many common terms and their medical equivalents, so you do not necessarily need to know the standard or established medical terminology when doing a search.

The best way to get accurate results on a topic is by using the MeSH term and its subheadings, not by trying to create a complex Boolean query yourself. For example, to look for *prevention and control of chronic mucocutaneous candidiasis*, it is best to browse for the MeSH term, then add the subheading *prevention and control* to the term. The search details will then be *Candidiasis, Chronic Mucocutaneous/prevention and control*.

When searching MeSH headings you do not have to list the terms as they appear in the MeSH tree structure. PubMed rearranges them as needed. For example, you can search for *interstitial nephritis* and the MeSH thesaurus will convert it to *nephritis, interstitial*. (Check this by clicking the Detail button after running a search.) In a similar fashion, the MeSH thesaurus will convert a phrase to its established terminology. When you search for *biliary cirrhosis*, PubMed converts this to *Liver Cirrhosis, Biliary*.

The MeSH browser is in active devlopment by the team working on PubMed, so expect changes in the future.

USE MESH MAJOR SUBJECT TO LIMIT A SEARCH

To find articles about emboli during hip surgery, what you are really looking for are articles where this is the *MeSH major subject*. The major subject is the point, the subject, the main purpose of the article. Remember that an article may have a dozen or two MeSH terms, but only two or three major subjects. To limit a search to a MeSH major subject, use the Advanced Search.

BECOME FAMILIAR WITH MEDLINE FIELDS

Become familiar with available search fields in MEDLINE. If you don't know that you can look for an author by name, you won't be able to limit a search to specific authors.

The first level of skill in searching MEDLINE is the ability to take a question phrased in natural language ("Has there been any research published in the last few years on side effects of ritalin therapy in young children?") and enter the question such that PubMed gives results. The second level of skill involves using the Modify Query fields to increase precision.

Learning to use MEDLINE is a matter of knowing when to run a broad search on All Fields, and when to limit a search by specific fields such as date, title word, publication type, or MeSH term.

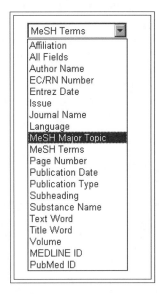

MEDLINE fields

PUBLICATION TYPES

After learning the MEDLINE fields and becoming familiar with the MeSH browser, take a look at the Publication Types in Appendix D. The following types may be especially useful: review of the literature, clinical trial, practice guideline. Know how to use the List Terms function in the Advance Search to look through a list of Publication Types.

TRICKS

SAVE A SEARCH

You can save a search as a Web page, then re-run the search again by opening that page.

1. Start from the Basic Search screen.

2. Enter your terms.

3. Use the browser's File, Save menu to save this page to your hard drive.

4. Use the browser's File, Open menu to open the saved page.

5. Create a bookmark to the version of the page on your hard drive.

To open and re-run the search:

1. Use the bookmark button or menu to open the page.

2. Click Search to re-run the search. This sends the request to PubMed.

INVESTIGATE DRUGS

Pharmaceuticals in MEDLINE are usually given the generic name, from the *Merck Index, International NonProprietary Names,* or *United States Adopted Names.* There are two strategies for looking up drugs.

One is to use Advanced Search with the Substance name field. Because this is so extensive, it is almost a companion to MeSH. Type the word (or partial word) and use List Terms to get a quick orientation to the terms and how many articles are available for a given drug. For example, by typing *ampho* I see immediately that there are about 4,600 articles related to Amphotericin B.

The second method uses the MeSH Browser's detailed display. With this you can discover how articles about a drug are sub-classified in MEDLINE. For example, after looking up *aspirin* in the MeSH browser, you can restrict your search to the following subheadings:

administration and dosage

adverse effects

analogs and derivatives

analysis

antagonists and inhibitors

blood

cerebrospinal fluid

chemical synthesis

chemistry

classification

contraindications

diagnostic use

economics

history

immunology

isolation and purification

metabolism

pharmacokinetics

pharmacology

physiology

poisoning

radiation effects

standards

supply and distribution

therapeutic use

toxicity

urine

You can also search for partial words or word fragments using the MeSH browser. If there is no exact match, for example if you search for *dimethyl*, the Browser will list all words that contain that fragment. The Browser will also connect word fragments intelligently with compounds; if you search for *nitro* it will include *nitric acid* and *nitrites* as well as *nitrofurantoin*.

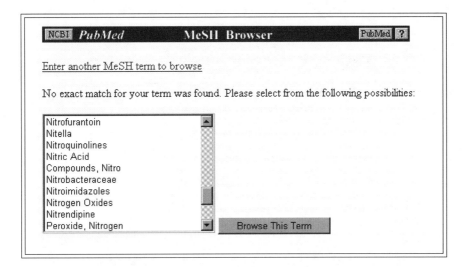

MeSH browser – partial word search

LOOK AT AGE GROUPS

MeSH includes the age of subjects in a study. You can limit a search to any of the following age ranges, using the MeSH Terms field:

Infant, Newborn	Birth to 1	month
Infant	1 – 23	months
Child, Preschool	2 – 5	years
Child	6 – 12	years
Adolescence	13 – 18	years
Adult	19 – 44	years
Middle age	45 – 64	years
Aged	65+	
Aged, 80 and over	79+	

Note that because MeSH terms are automatically exploded, a search on Child will include Infant through Adolescence.

GENERATE A TABLE OF CONTENTS

You can use the Citation Matcher to generate a table of contents for an issue of a journal. Enter the journal title, year, volume and issue number.

PubMed

Citation Matcher for Single Articles

Enter information about the article you wish to find.

Journal: american journal of orthopedics

Date: 1998

Volume: 27   Issue: 3   First page:

Author's last name and initials (e.g., Smith BJ)

Search   Clear

Using Citation Matcher to generate a table of contents

SEARCH FOR ARTICLES ABOUT A PERSON

This is possible because PubMed has a field for "personal author as subject." To find articles about C. E. Koop, type `Koop[ps]` in either the Basic or Advanced Search form.

Thanks to PubMed's pull-down menus, you do not have to learn a complicated computer syntax. However, not all the fields in MEDLINE are currently searchable this way. You *can* search the remainder of the two-letter fields, known as category qualifiers, by typing a word and then placing the two-letter qualifier in brackets. See Appendix D for a list of two-letter category qualifiers.

SEARCH FOR ARTICLES RELATED TO AN INSTITUTION

Because the Affiliation field contains information on the institution with which the primary author is affiliated, you can look for research done by or through a particular university or research center, such as the Mayo Clinic or the American Heart Association.

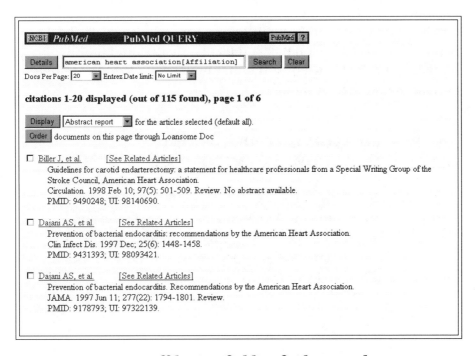

**Using Affiliation field to find research
related to an institution**

FIND A SECONDARY AUTHOR

If you are looking for persons who have worked on a particular piece of research, but who are not the primary author, MEDLINE will still help. At the current time up to twenty-five authors are included in the Author field for each citation, so you can search for secondary authors and research assistants as well as main authors. In the past the rules have varied in terms of how many authors for an article would be included:

1966-1984	all authors
1985-1996	first ten authors
1996+	first twenty-five authors

If there are more than twenty-five authors, the first twenty-four and the last will be included.

Names are transliterated from Cyrillic and other non-Roman alphabets such as Chinese and Japanese. Diacritical marks such as those found with these letters – á ê ñ – are not included in PubMed, but can be found in printed Index Medicus.

Remember in searching for authors to use the format *smith pa*, where smith is the last name and pa are the first and middle initial. You can also use just the first initial, for example *smith p*, or just the last name: *smith*.

USE PARTIAL WORDS (TRUNCATION)
IF YOU DON'T KNOW AN ENTIRE TERM

Don't remember how to spell a word? Use the List Terms mode and an asterisk (*) to have PubMed remind you. For example, if you are looking for `hemorrhoid` but can't remember how to spell it, use the Advanced Search page with List Terms, type `hemor*` andPubMed will show you the correct term.

8
THE INNER WORKINGS
OF PUBMED

BASIC SEARCH

This chapter explains some of the programming behind PubMed. You certainly don't need to know any of this, and if you are in a hurry you can skip this chapter without missing anything you need to do a search. But if you are wondering what happens when you look for a term in Basic Search, or how a Clinical Query is carried out, or how the See Related Articles function compares articles for similarity, read on.

1. PubMed looks at its index to see if the term is a MeSH heading. If so, it searches the MeSH term OR the text word.

2. If it isn't a MeSH term, it compares it to two *translation tables* until a match is found. Thus, a search on *bleeding* looks in the tables, finds the standard MeSH term *hemorrhage*, and a complex search is created automatically: ("Hemorrhage"[MeSH Terms] OR bleeding[Text Word]).

3. If PubMed can't find a MeSH equivalent, it looks at the Journal table to see if there is a journal by that name. A search on *cell proliferation* finds the journal *Cell Proliferation*, since there is no MeSH phrase with these two words.

4. If PubMed can't find a journal, it looks in a list of phrases. For example, the phrase *heart attack* is automatically translated to *myocardial infarction.*

5. If PubMed can't find a phrase, and one of the terms has a one- or two-letter word after it (jones pa), PubMed tries the Author index.

6. If PubMed can't find an author, it then tries variations on the word order.

7. As a last resort, PubMed takes every individual word and runs them through the translation table, phrase list, and author index.

SEE RELATED ARTICLES

This function in PubMed is useful for conducting a rapid literature search. What is PubMed doing when it searches for related articles?

Contrary to what you might expect, PubMed does *not* run a search at the time you click See Related Articles. Instead, the database periodically goes through the algorithm outlined below and generates a list of all the articles related to each citation. Then when you look for Related Articles, it uses this precompiled list.

The algorithm compares the similarity in title, abstract, and MeSH terms for the article in question to all the other articles in PubMed. In step by step fashion, PubMed does the following:

1. Stop words are eliminated.

2. A limited amount of stemming is done.

3. Words are classified into three categories: text word, title word, and MeSH term.
   a. Words in the abstract are classified as text words.
   b. Title words are classified as both text and title words.

c. MeSH terms are placed in that category, and MeSH terms with a subheading are classified under the generic term and the term/subheading pair. MeSH major terms are classified both as MeSH and MeSH major term.

4. Each word is assigned a global weight, depending on the number of articles with that word and how important the word is in determining relationships. Global weight is higher for rare words, lower for common ones.

5. Each word is assigned a local weight, depending on how often it appears in the particular article.

6. The similarity between the article and every other article in the database is computed:
    a. The formula (local weight x local weight x global weight) is calculated for all terms the two documents have in common.
    b. This product is divided by the product of the lengths of the two documents, producing a vector cosine score.

7. A list of articles with the highest score (those which are most similar) is compiled and saved.

CLINICAL QUERIES

The Clinical Queries are really just pre-written searches, using MeSH terms and subheadings, on research studies and methodology. This allows you to do a quick search using terms with which you are familiar (therapy, diagnosis, etiology, prognosis, sensitivity, specificity).

The expanded phrases below show the syntax that PubMed adds to your term when you run a Clinical Query. These are MeSH terms and subheadings which narrow the search to the general area of therapy, etc. In each case, the entire phrase is connected by Boolean AND to the term(s) you are searching for. Parentheses are used to show the ordering of elements in the search syntax; brackets are used for the [no explosion] parameter when used with MeSH subheadings. To make the syntax somewhat more understandable, I have put each phrase on a separate line, but in reality they are complete phrases.

As an example, when searching for the word *gentamycin*, with a focus on *therapy* and *sensitivity*, the syntax would begin:

gentamycin AND ((publication type *randomized controlled trial...* etc.

Therapy + sensitivity

((publication type *randomized controlled trial* OR MeSH subheading *drug therapy*)

OR MeSH subheading [no explosion] *therapeutic use*)

OR text word *random*

Therapy + specificity

(text word *double* AND text word *blind*)

OR text word *placebo*

Diagnosis + sensitivity

(MeSH term *sensitivity and specificity* OR Text word *sensitivity*)

OR (MeSH subheading *diagnosis* OR MeSH subheading *diagnostic use*)

OR Text word *specificity*

Diagnosis + specificity

MeSH term *sensitivity and specificity*

OR (text word *predictive* AND text word *value*)

Etiology + sensitivity

(MeSH term *cohort studies* OR MeSH term *risk*)

OR (text word *odds* AND text word *ratio*)

OR (text word *relative* AND text word *risk*)

OR (text word *case* AND text word *control*)

Etiology + specificity

MeSH term [no explosion] *case-control studies*

OR MeSH term [no explosion] *cohort studies*

Prognosis + sensitivity

((((((MeSH term *incidence* OR MeSH term *mortality* OR MeSH term *follow-up studies*) OR MeSH subheading *mortality*) OR text word *prosnos**) OR text word *predict**) OR text word *course*)

Prognosis + specificity

MeSH term [no explosion] *prognosis* OR MeSH term [no explosion] *survival analysis*

For example, the Clinical Query choices for Etiology, with a focus on specificity, limit your search with two MeSH terms: *case-control studies* and *cohort studies*. In other words, the way that health professionals understand and use the term *etiology* matches closes with these two MeSH terms which the staff of the NLM assign to citations.

9

DOCUMENT DELIVERY

LOANSOME DOC

Not everyone has immediate access to a medical library. After finding a citation, how do you obtain and read the entire article?

The National Library of Medicine has a document ordering service called Loansome Doc. This service is not free; once you have set it up, you pay each time you want to receive an article. To use Loansome Doc you have to do the following:

1. obtain the identification number for a specific medical library

2. register for Loansome Doc using PubMed or Internet Grateful Med

3. order articles using PubMed

REGISTER FOR THE SERVICE AT YOUR LOCAL MEDICAL LIBRARY

See Appendix A or call 1-800-338-7657 for a list of medical libraries with library identification numbers. The NN/LM comprises more than 140 Resource Libraries (mostly at medical schools) and 4,500 Primary Access Libraries (mostly at hospitals).

Electronic delivery using the Internet, requires the local library
to have special software and hardware for scanning documents
and converting them to electronic form. Once
you have set up the arrangement, the electronic version of a
document can be sent to you as an attachment to an email
message. Not many libraries have this capability yet, so be
sure to ask. This method uses two programs, Ariel
http://www.rlg.org/ariel.html, a program developed by Research
Libraries Group for scanning or viewing, and DocView
http://archive.nlm.nih.gov/proj/docview/factsht.htm for retrieving
or printing. You can download DocView for free from the NLM.

REGISTERING FOR LOANSOME DOC

Once you have the identification number for a local library,
use the main Loansome Doc page
http://tendon.nlm.nih.gov/ld/loansome.html and click on
Registration. You will then see the following page.

The library ID is the number you must request from your local
library.

NLM	Loansome Doc Registration

IDENTIFICATION INFORMATION

Ordering
Library ID : [____] (required)
First Name : [_____]
Last Name : [_____] (required)

ADDRESS INFORMATION

Address 1 : [_____] (required)
Address 2 : [_____]
City : [_____] (required)
Province/State : [_____▼] (U.S. and Canada Only)
Province/State : [_____] (International Only)
Country : [_____▼]
Postal Code : [_____] (required)
Phone : [_____] (required)

DELIVERY INFORMATION

Loansome Doc registration

At the bottom of this page you enter information on how you wish articles to be delivered, as well as your login name and password which you will use when ordering articles. You can have articles delivered: by mail, fax, electronically, or you can pick them up at the library yourself.

```
                         DELIVERY INFORMATION

         Method :   ⦿ Mail   ○ Fax   ○ Pickup   ○ Internet Address
Forward Requests ?  ⦿ No      ○ Yes

            Fax : [                    ]

Internet Address : [                                            ]

  Requester Note : [                                            ]

                          LOGIN INFORMATION
                 Use for all future Loansome Doc orders.

        User ID : [                    ] (required)

       Password : [          ] (required)

Retype Password : [          ] (required)

  [ Register ]
```

Loansome Doc registration – delivery information

ORDERING ARTICLES FROM LOANSOME DOC

After running a search in PubMed, you see a list of citations on the Document List screen. (See Chapter 3 for a view of the Document List screen). At the top and bottom of this screen is an Order button which you use to order articles.

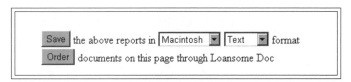

Order button

- Check the box next to the articles that you wish to order, then click the **Order** button.

On the next screen you enter your login and password which you created during registration.

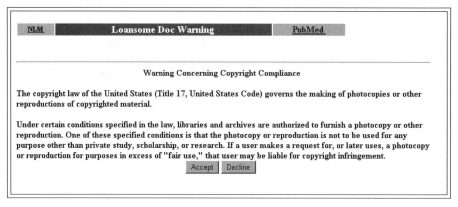

Loansome Doc login

After login you are shown a copyright notice.

Copyright notice

Next you will see the order screen.

- Click **Send Order**. You may also add a note in the box to the right of **Requester Note**.

NLM	**Loansome Doc Order**	PubMed

Send Order

Print or save a copy of this page for reference.
Please confirm ordering of the following documents:

☑ · 98296949 Is it heart attack, or is it GERD?
Adv Nurse Pract 1998 May; 6(5):57-58

Delivery Information

Method	⦿ Mail ○ Fax ○ Pickup ○ Internet Address
Not Needed After (yyyymmdd)	
Forward Requests ?	⦿ No ○ Yes
Requester Note	

User Information:

User ID:

United States
Email:
Library: 95616B UNIVERSITY OF CALIFORNIA AT DAVIS CARLSON HEALTH SCIENCES
LIBRARY/DAVIS CA
Date: 06/25/98

Order screen

At the bottom of this screen, under User Information, will be your name and other contact information that you entered when you registered with Loansome Doc.

Finally, you are shown a confirmation screen.

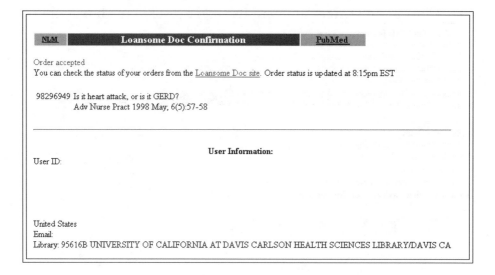

Confirmation screen

You can check the status of your order at

http://tendon.nlm.nih.gov/ld/loansome.html

by entering your login and password.

OTHER DOCUMENT DELIVERY SERVICES

Loansome Doc is administered through the NLM, but there are many other services. Some are commercial, others are administered through universities. See Appendix C for a list, or go to *http://www.nnlm.nlm.nih.gov/pnr/docsupp*

Rates vary from $10-25 per article depending on the service and type of delivery requested.

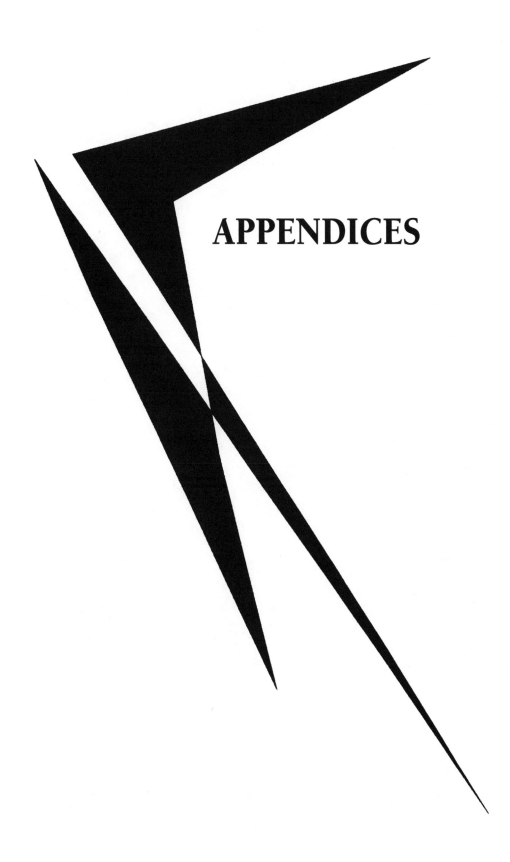

APPENDICES

A NATIONAL LIBRARY OF MEDICINE

LIBRARY CATALOGS AND HUMAN KNOWLEDGE

Library catalogs organize books and other materials in some kind of order, so they can be arranged in a collection and retrieved easily. Classification, on the other hand, assigns a category, such as *fiction*, to an item. In addition to books, a library needs to keep track of magazines, audio tapes, videos, individual papers, government documents, dissertations, music scores, and much else. In effect, this organizes the entire structure of human knowledge. Two widely used methods are the Dewey Decimal and the Library of Congress systems.

DEWEY DECIMAL SYSTEM

Used by more than 135 countries, the Dewey system is the most common library classification system in the world; it is in use by approximately 95% of public and school library catalogs in the United States. The Dewey system was conceived by Melvil Dewey in 1873. Prior to that time, books were given a number that corresponded to their location on the shelves - each book in each library had a fixed location. This method didn't allow for growth of a library's collection, or for finding a book by subject. Dewey's system enabled both of these. Today the Dewey Decimal System is maintained by the Online Computer Library Center, Inc. (OCLC- *http://www.oclc.org*), which links more than 26,000 libraries around the world, and maintains the largest online catalog, WorldCat, with 38 million records in 400 languages.

The decimal system organizes all knowledge into classes and subclasses, using a decimal notation. There are ten classes, each of which has ten subclasses, and so on. Thus any class or item can be written numerically.

LIBRARY OF CONGRESS

The United States Library of Congress was established as a legislative library on April 24, 1800. Its principal founder, Thomas Jefferson, believed that a democratic legislature needed information and ideas to do its work. Two years later, the president and vice-president were allowed to borrow books. Today, the library houses more than 100 million items, 20 million of which are books.

The Library of Congress classifies its materials into 21 categories, assigning a letter to each one. Subclasses are given combinations of letters, and further subtopics are given a numerical notation.

MEDICAL BOOKS AND JOURNALS

Within the Library of Congress classification, several letters are reserved for medical subjects. The letter R contains general medical subjects, and the letters QS through QZ describe pre-clinical subjects. In addition, the letter W was given to the National Library of Medicine for its own use. Medical journals are catalogued under the letter *W* and the number *1*. They are arranged alphabetically in the stacks, by title of the publication.

CARD CATALOGS AND DATABASES

The card for every item in a library contains author, title, and subject information. Such a physical system is limited. Books and articles can be classified in many other ways than just author, title, and subject. What about year of publication? Or name of the publisher? And how many cross-references can be added to a subject catalog before it becomes too cumbersome to maintain?

Computerized databases such as MEDLINE are the answer to this need to maintain and manage more and more pieces of information. In addition to the basic database structure, MEDLINE incorporates an 18,000-word thesaurus and hierarchy (MeSH) which enables a wide range of ways to search for a subject.

INDEX MEDICUS

In 1865 Dr. John Shaw Billings was assigned to the post of Surgeon General of the Army of the United States, and he set about to create a comprehensive library of medical literature. After eight years he had accumulated 50,000 volumes, and to keep track of them all he devised an index for the books and a periodical index for the journals. In 1880 the first edition of *Index Medicus* was published under the title *Index Catalog of the Library of the Surgeon General's Office*. Since then it has been continuously published. The *Index* comes out monthly, and is compiled annually and published as the *Cumulated Index Medicus*.

Index Medicus is a citation index to medical literature. In other words, it contains citations to articles from medical journals.

Currently, references to over 3,000 journals from around the world are included in *Index Medicus,* and more are added each year. Smaller pieces such as letters to the editor and editorials are also referenced. If a journal covers other subjects, only those articles that apply to biomedicine are included in the *Index.*

NLM AND NN/LM

The National Library of Medicine (NLM) is part of the National Institutes of Health, located in Bethesda, Maryland. Its mission:

> "The National Library of Medicine collects, organizes, and disseminates the biomedical literature of the world in order to advance the medical and related sciences and to improve the public health. The Library serves as a national information resource for research, health care, the education of health professionals, and service activities of Federal and private agencies, organizations, institutions, and individuals."

The NLM collection houses more than five million items, including historical and rare texts. Through the National Network of Libraries of Medicine (NN/LM) the NLM strives to make medical information available to all health professionals. The NN/LM serves as a resource for regional and local medical libraries through 8 Regional Medical Libraries, 140 Resource Libraries, and more than 4,500 Primary Access Libraries. In addition to reference information, the NN/LM maintains a training center, provides interlibrary loans, and assists with MEDLINE. The NN/LM Web site about PubMed

http://www.nnlm.nlm.nih.gov/nnlm/online

is probably the best place to find detailed tutorials and explanations about MEDLINE and PubMed.

Today the National Library of Medicine is the largest medical library in the world, with an annual budget of more than $161 million. It is involved in such innovative projects as the Visible Human, telemedicine, and the creation of digital libraries. It provides research support and grants for Internet access, computer technology, information management, informatics training, and manuscript preparation and publication.

MEDLARS

In 1960 the National Library of Medicine started work on a computerized system to keep track of medical literature. Called MEDLARS (Medical Literature Analysis and Retrieval System), this now comprises various computer systems (ELHILL, Toxnet, and PDQ), over forty databases, and eighteen million references, all of which are available online. Though most items are bibliographic citations to literature, some of the MEDLARS databases contain other types of information, such as lists of clinical trials for AIDS patients. A few of these databases are available through Internet Grateful Med, but most require you to register with the NLM, obtain a user identification code, and then be charged for their use. For most non-Web types of access you are billed as well. (The AIDS databases, however, are free for searching through Internet Grateful Med.)

Before you can access the different MEDLARS databases you need to obtain a user ID and password. Online registration is available at *https://access.nlm.nih.gov*. After you register, you can telnet to *medlars.nlm.nih.gov* or use telecommunications software to dial directly to 1-800-525-0216. (If you dial directly, you may need to set some parameters on your modem program so that your modem is operating in the same way as the modem you will be dialing into. Modem programs typically have a Settings screen where these choices can be made. For direct dialing, modem configuration should be 7 data bits, 1 stop bit, even parity, full duplex, and a speed of 1200, 2400 or 9600 bps.)

Charges depend upon the amount of time you are connected, the number of citations you download, how many search statements you submit, and the amount of work the computer does to run your searches. There are no minimums, and if you don't do any searches you are not charged any monthly fees. The NLM estimates that the average search costs $1.25-$5.00. For more information, see ***http://www.nlm.nih.gov/databases/leased.html.***

PREMEDLINE

A PubMed search includes the PreMEDLINE database as well as MEDLINE. Before articles reach MEDLINE, they are placed into the temporary database called PreMEDLINE. MeSH terms have not yet been assigned, so these citations will not show up in a search which is limited to a MeSH term. But they are searchable by author, title, and abstract words. A PreMEDLINE citation in PubMed will have the following tag: [MEDLINE record in progress]. Because the citations from a basic PubMed search are displayed in the order in which they have been added to the database (most recent first), you will often see a dozen or more PreMEDLINE citations at the beginning of the list.

MEDLINE

MEDLINE indexes approximately 3,900 journals, many more than are found in *Index Medicus.* It includes journals from other lists, such as the *Hospital and Health Administration Index,* the *Index to Dental Literature*, and the *International Nursing Index.* (The complete list of journals, approximately 400 pages, is available for download from the Internet.) Some journals have a broad subject area, but also contain medical articles. MEDLINE selectively indexes only the citations for medical and health articles from those journals. (However, if a publisher supplies the entire set of citations electronically, these all go into MEDLINE.)

MEDLINE considers journals which fall into the areas of research, clinical observations, analysis, discussion or analysis of health care, critical reviews, statistical compilations, evaluations of methods or procedures, and case reports. MEDLINE usually does not include journals which are limited to reprints, abstracts, news, book reviews, or journals that report activities of associations. The mix of journals changes over time, and the NLM has recently added several consumer health titles such as the *Harvard Health Letter* in response to increased use of MEDLINE by the public. MEDLINE even includes journals that are published online, such as the *Online Journal of Current Clinical Trials.*

PreMEDLINE is updated daily. MEDLINE is updated weekly; the new citations are available on Saturdays. Approximately 7,000 new citations are added each week, or 350,000 per year.

In addition to the current database, MEDLINE contains Backfile databases which cover five year time periods. (The earliest and the most recent databases cover other ranges of years.) PubMed searches the entire set of databases by default, unless you limit the search to recent years. When using other interfaces to MEDLINE (such as Ovid or Silverplatter) some will search only the most recent years, not the entire set from 1966 to the present. The names and approximate number of citations in each Backfile are shown below:

Med66	1966-1974	1.9	million citations
Med75	1975-1979	1.3	
Med80	1980-1984	1.4	
Med85	1985-1989	1.7	
Med90	1990-1992	1.1	
Med93	1993-1994	0.7	

Institutions in the United States can lease the MEDLARS databases on magnetic tape; in addition, public institutions in foreign countries can be designated as International MEDLARS Centers. There are no user charges after the initial lease. The data supplied is on 3480 tape cartridges or 6250 BPI 9-track tape, EBCDIC with standard IBM labeling. The current year and backfile databases are leased separately; the current year's MEDLINE is $5,000-$9,000, and backfile databases range from $1,750 - $7,000. Note that the databases do not include any search software - this must be developed or purchased separately. Sample tapes can be obtained for $50, in order to determine if your institution has the software and technical expertise to work with the databases.

NCBI, ENTREZ, AND PUBMED

The <u>N</u>ational <u>C</u>enter for <u>B</u>iotechnology <u>I</u>nformation was established at the NLM in 1988 to develop new information technologies. The NCBI developed a system called Entrez to allow integrated searching for DNA and protein sequences, genome mapping, three-dimensional protein structures, and bibliographic citations. Entrez is the retrieval software used for PubMed. NCBI maintains a set of search screens for nucleotides, proteins, which can be found at ***http://www.ncbi.nlm.nih.gov/Entrez***.

Entrez

Search WWW Entrez at NCBI

- Nucleotides
- Proteins
- 3D structures
- Genomes
- Taxonomy
- Literature - PubMed

The Entrez Browser is provided by the National Center for Biotechnology Information. NCBI also builds, maintains, and distributes the GenBank Sequence Database.

Entrez Help

The Entrez Databases

Network Entrez

Retrieve large
data sets

Making WWW
Links to Entrez

Entrez

These databases contain fields specific to biotechnology, such as organism, sequence length, or protein name.

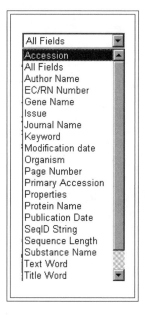

Entrez search fields

PubMed was opened to the public on June 26, 1997. In January 1998 version 2.0 added the MeSH browser, gave access to the Loansome Doc retrieval from PubMed, and upgraded the Citation Matcher.

In summary, the PubMed site uses the Entrez search engine to access the PubMed database, which in turn is drawn from MEDLINE and PreMEDLINE.

UMLS

The variety of classification systems in use with medical information is not always apparent to health professionals. We work at the level of medical vocabulary. (A rosacea is a rosacea is a rosacea, the world round.) Despite the standardization of everyday medical vocabulary (e.g. terms such as *fibromyalgia* or *osteoporosis*), there are more than forty schemes for organizing medical information, ranging from the widely known and used International Classification of Diseases (ICD) or Current Procedural Terminology (CPT codes), to lesser known vocabularies such as DXplain, developed by Massachusetts General Hospital, or the Standard Product Nomenclature of the Federal Drug Administration. How does a person (or a computer program) do a search using two or more systems, which may involve different terms, concepts, and relationships?

To solve the problem of finding or using information from a variety of sources, in 1986 the NLM began work on the Unified Medical Language System (UMLS). The UMLS keeps track of and integrates information from these forty different classification systems.

The UMLS is continually developing four different computer databases, called "knowledge sources." One is a *Metathesaurus* of terms, synonyms and relationships; another is a *Semantic Network* relating each term to a category; the third is a *Specialist Lexicon* and the fourth is an *Information Sources Map* which describes the different databases and systems where information can be found. Together these comprise an evolving set of tools to enable more intelligent and comprehensive use of medical information.

Machine-readable forms of the different UMLS products are freely available for companies or institutions to use in developing search tools. At the current time these knowledge sources include more than 450,000 concepts and one million names, linked together in a variety of ways (synonyms, variations, translations, syntactical category), and logical relationships (e.g., heart attack is a synonym for myocardial infarction; icterus is a variation of the term jaundice; ptca translates to percutaneous coronary transluminal angioplasty; ampicillin belongs in the category of antibiotics).

Examples of Web sites which use portions of the UMLS are CliniWeb *http://www.ohsu.edu/cliniweb* and Medical World Search *http://www.mwsearch.com*. Dr. William Detmer, a leader in the field of medical informatics, has developed a prototype

called Medweaver
http://www.med.Virginia.edu/~wmd4n/medweaver.html
which uses UMLS to assist decisions (diagnoses), search
MEDLINE, and find Web sites.

VOYAGER

The National Library of Medicine is about to undertake a major
change, moving from a mainframe to a client-server computer
system. The new system, produced by Endeavor Information
Systems *http://www.endinfosys.com*, is called Voyager. It is a
relational database and can be used to create an online public
access catalog through several means such as the Web and telnet.
Voyager uses the standard protocol for searching library catalogs
(Z39.50) and will probably become the standard interface for
finding texts and other materials at the National Library of
Medicine. A number of new functions will become available,
such as linking to a Web resource for a citation, checking the
loan status of a book, and downloading search results. The NLM
expects Voyager to be available in the fall of 1998.

THE FUTURE OF PUBMED

The PubMed interface undergoes continual improvement.
Changes planned for the near future include enabling limits on
the Advanced Search page. There will also be more options for
displaying citations, and the ability to sort the results of a search
by journal title. Finally, there will be the ability to store your
individual preferences. Preferences may include search strategies
or printing methods.

HOW TO CONTACT THE NLM

The National Library of Medicine has central contact points for questions about any of its services.

Phone	888-FINDNLM (888-346-3656)
Fax	301-496-0822
Email	custserv@nlm.nih.gov
Address	8600 Rockville Pike, Bethesda, MD 20894

REGIONAL AND INTERNATIONAL MEDICAL LIBRARIES

These are libraries with which you can establish a document delivery agreement. The cost varies with each library. The individual web sites for each regional library are also a good source for training materials, Internet resources, and contacts.

For more information, call the National Network of Libraries of Medicine at 1-800-338-7657.

The most up-to-date version of this list is available at:
http://www.nlm.nih.gov/pubs/factsheets/nnlm.html

MIDDLE ATLANTIC REGION

The New York Academy of Medicine
1216 Fifth Avenue
New York, New York 10029
Phone: (212) 822-7396
Fax: (212) 534-7042
URL: http://www.nnlm.nlm.nih.gov/mar
States Served: DE, NJ, NY, PA
NATIONAL ONLINE CENTER FOR ALL REGIONS

SOUTHEASTERN/ATLANTIC REGION

University of Maryland at Baltimore
Health Sciences Library
601 West Lombard Street
Baltimore, Maryland 21201-1583
Phone: (410) 706-2855
Fax: (410) 706-0099
URL: http://www.nnlm.nlm.nih.gov/sar
States Served: AL, FL, GA, MD, MS, NC, SC, TN, VA,
WV, the District of Columbia, Puerto Rico, and the U.S.
Virgin Islands

GREATER MIDWEST REGION

The University of Illinois at Chicago
Library of the Health Sciences (M/C 763)
1750 W. Polk Street
Chicago, Illinois 60612-7223
Phone: (312) 996-2464
Fax: (312) 996-2226
URL: http://www.nnlm.nlm.nih.gov/gmr
States Served: IA, IL, IN, KY, MI, MN, ND, OH, SD, WI

MIDCONTINENTAL REGION

University of Nebraska Medical Center
Leon S. McGoogan Library of Medicine
600 South 42nd Street
Omaha, Nebraska 68198-6706
Phone: (402) 559-4326
Fax: (402) 559-5482
URL: http://www.nnlm.nlm.nih.gov/mr
States Served: CO, KS, MO, NE, UT, WY

SOUTH CENTRAL REGION

Houston Academy of Medicine-
Texas Medical Center Library
1133 M.D. Anderson Boulevard
Houston, Texas 77030-2809
Phone: (713) 799-7880
Fax: (713) 790-7030
Internet: nnlmscr@library.tmc.edu
URL: http://www.nnlm.nlm.nih.gov/scr
States Served: AR, LA, NM, OK, TX

PACIFIC NORTHWEST REGION

Health Sciences Libraries and Information Center
Box 357155
University of Washington
Seattle, Washington 98195-7155
Phone: (206) 543-8262
Fax: (206) 543-2469
Internet: nnlm@u.washington.edu
URL: http://www.nnlm.nlm.nih.gov/pnr
States Served: AK, ID, MT, OR, WA

PACIFIC SOUTHWEST REGION

University of California, Los Angeles
Louise M. Darling Biomedical Library
12-077 Center for the Health Sciences
Box 951798
Los Angeles, California 90095-1798
Phone: (310) 825-1200
Fax: (310) 825-5389
URL: http://www.nnlm.nlm.nih.gov/psr
States Served: AZ, CA, HI, NV, and U.S. Territories in
the Pacific Basin

NEW ENGLAND REGION

University of Connecticut Health Center
Lyman Maynard Stowe Library
263 Farmington Avenue
Farmington, Connecticut 06030-5370
Phone: (860) 679-4500
Fax: (860) 679-1305
URL: http://www.nnlm.nlm.nih.gov/ner
States Served: CT, MA, ME, NH, RI, VT

INTERNATIONAL MEDLARS CENTERS

AUSTRALIA

National Library of Australia
Canberra ACT 2603, Australia
Telephone: 61-6-262-1326
FAX: 61-6-273-1180
e-mail: m.newman@nla.gov.au
Web site: http://www.nla.gov.au

CANADA

Canada Institute for Scientific and
Technical Information (CISTI)
National Research Council of Canada
Ottawa, Ontario KIA OS2
Canada
Telephone: 1-800-668-1222
FAX: 613-952-8244
e-mail: cisti.medlars@nrc.ca
Web site: http://www.cisti.nrc.ca/ cisti/cisti.html

CHINA

Institute of Medical Information
Chinese Academy of Medical Sciences
3, Yabao Road, Choyang District
Beijing 10002, China
Telephone: 8610-512-8185
FAX: 8610-512-8176
e-mail: wangrk@bepc2.ihep.ac.cn
Web site: http://www.imicams.ac.cn

EGYPT
ENSTINET

Academy of Scientific Research and Technology
P.O. Box 1522, Attaba 11511
Cairo, Egypt
Telephone: 202-355-7253
FAX: 202-354-7807
e-mail: ab@enstinet.eg.net
Web site: http://www.sti.sci.eg

FRANCE
INSERM

101, rue de Tolbiac
75654 Paris Cedex 13
France
Telephone: 33-1-44-23-60-70
FAX: 33-1-44-23-60-99
e-mail: advocat@inserm-dicdoc.u-strasbg.fr
Web site: http://www-inserm.u-strasbg.fr

GERMANY

Deutsches Institute for Medical
Documentation and Information (DIMDI)
Postfach 420580, D-50899
Koln, Germany
Telephone: 49-221-472-4252
FAX: 49-221-41-1429
Web site: http://www.dimdi.de

HONG KONG

The Chinese University of Hong Kong
Prince of Wales Hospital
Li Ping Medical Library
Shantin, N.T., Hong Kong
Telephone: 852-2632-2466
FAX: 852-2637-7817
e-mail: medref@cuhk.edu.hk
Web site: http://www.lib.cuhk.hk/medlib/ mdmain.htm

INDIA

National Informatics Center
Planning Commission
A-Block, CGO Complex, Lodi Road
New Delhi 110003, India
Telephone: 91-11-436-2359
FAX: 91-11-436-2628
e-mail: root@medlar0.delhi.nic.in

ISRAEL

Hebrew University, Hadassah Medical
School Berman National Medical Library
P.O. Box 12272
Jerusalem 91120, Israel
Telephone: 972-2-675-8795
FAX: 972-2-675-8376
e-mail: ester@mdlib.huji.ac.il

ITALY

Ministry of Health
Istituto Superiore di Sanita
Viale Regina Elena 299
00161 Rome, Italy
Telephone: 39-6-499-2280
FAX: 39-6-444-0246
e-mail: dracos@net.iss.it
Web site: http://www.iss.it

JAPAN

Japan Science and Technology Corporation (JST)
Information Center for Science and Technology
Department of Service
5-3, Yonbancho,
Chiyoda-ku, Tokyo 102-0081 Japan
Telephone: 81-3-5214-8411
FAX: 81-3-5214-8410
Web site: http://www.jst.go.jp/

KOREA

Medical Library
Seoul National University
College of Medicine
28 Yongon-dong, Chongno-gu
Seoul 110-799, Korea
Telephone: 822-740-8044
FAX: 822-762-5363
Web site: http://solarsnet.snu.ac.kr/ medlib/kor_med_center.htm

KUWAIT

Ministry of Public Health
Kuwait Institute for Medical Specialization
P.O. Box 1793 Safat
Code 13018, Kuwait
Telephone: 965-247-2210
FAX: 965-241-0028

MEXICO

Centro Nacional de Informacion y Documentacion
sobre Salud (CENIDS)
Leibnitz # 20, 3er, piso, Colonia Anzures
Delegacion Benito Juarez
11590 Mexico D.F., Mexico
Telephone: 525-563-27-82
FAX: 525-598-21-78
e-mail: gladys@cenids.ssa.gob.mx
Web site: http://www.ssa.gob.mx/

RUSSIA

The State Central Scientific Medical Library
30, Krasikova St.
117418, Moscow, Russia
Telephone: 7-095-128-33-46
FAX: 7-095-128-87-39
e-mail: loginov@server.scsml.rssi.ru

SOUTH AFRICA

South African Medical Research Council
P.O. Box 19070
Tygerberg 7505, South Africa
Telephone: 27-21-938-0219
FAX: 27-21-938-0201
e-mail: jalouw@eagle.mrc.ac.za
Web site: http://www.mrc.ac.za

SWEDEN

Karolinska Institute Library
PO Box 200
S-171-77 Stockholm, Sweden
Telephone: 46-8-728-8000
FAX: 46-8-330-0481
e-mail: goran.falkenberg@micforum.ki.se
Web site: http://www.kib.ki.se

SWITZERLAND

Documentation Service of the
Swiss Academy of Medical Sciences
Effingerstrasse 40
P.O. Box 5921, 3001 Bern
Switzerland
Telephone: 41-31-389 92 22
FAX: 41-31-389 92 45
e-mail: dokdi@sams.ch
Web site: http://www.sams.ch

UNITED KINGDOM

The British Library
Boston Spa, Wetherby
West Yorkshire LS23 7BQ
United Kingdom
Telephone: 44-1-937-546364
FAX: 44-1-937-546458
e-mail: blink-helpdesk@bl.uk
Web site: http://www.bl.uk/

PAN AMERICAN HEALTH ORGANIZATION

(PAHO) Headquarters, Room 854
525 Twenty-third Street, N.W.
Washington, D.C. 20037
Telephone: 202-861-3212
FAX: 202 223-5971
e-mail: gamboa@nlm.nih.gov
Web site: http://www.bireme.br/

BIREME/PAHO

Centro Latino Americano e de Caribe
Informcao em Ciencias da Saude
Organizacao Pan-Americana da Saude
Rua Botucatu 862
Vila Clementino
04023, SP-901
Sao Paulo, Brazil
Telephone: 55-11-549-2611
FAX: 55-11-571-1919
e-mail: celia@bireme.br
Web site: http://www.bireme.br/

INTERGOVERNMENTAL ORGANIZATION

Science and Technology Information
Center 106, Sec. 2, Ho-Ping E. Rd.
Taipei 10636, Taiwan
Telephone: 886-2-737-7690
FAX: 886-2-737-7664
e-mail: sheu@mail.stic.gov.tw
Web site: http://192.83.171.250/

CLASSES AND TRAINING MATERIALS

The best information on PubMed and MEDLINE is available
directly from the National Library of Medicine, including their
excellent *PubMed Training Guides*. For links, go to the *Reviews,
guides and factsheets* list from the National Network of Libraries
of Medicine. For a complete list of publications available for
purchase from the NLM, see

http://wwwindex.nlm.nih.gov/pubs/pubcat.html

The NN/LM maintains the National Online Training Center at
the New York Academy of Medicine. For a current description of
classes, locations, and schedules, see

http://www.nnlm.nlm.nih.gov/mar/online

Classes from the NN/LM are free. They are intended mainly for
health librarians and information specialists. You can register
online, or by fax or mail. Registration is not available by phone.

National Online Training Center NN/LM
1216 Fifth Avenue
New York, NY 10029
FAX: 212-534-7042
Phone: 212-822-7396 or 800-338-7657

The National Library of Medicine distributes free materials via
the Internet. These cover PubMed, Internet Grateful Med, MED-
LARS, ELHILL, and Boolean search hints. Some of these are
available as Powerpoint slide shows directly from the Internet, or
as pdf files that can be downloaded and printed.

The entire training manual used in the NN/LM courses above is freely available online for printing. This manual is more than 100 pages, and covers much of the same material as this book. I highly recommend it. The manual is available in pdf, postscript, or WordPerfect.

http://www.nlm.nih.gov/pubs/web_based.html

MEDLARS DATABASES

ELHILL DATABASES

AIDSDRUGS

Substances being tested in AIDS-related clinical trials

AIDSLINE

Acquired immunodeficiency syndrome (AIDS) and related topics

AIDSTRIALS

Clinical trials of substances being tested for use against AIDS, HIV infection, and AIDS-related opportunistic diseases

AVLINE

Biomedical audiovisual materials and computer software

BIOETHICSLINE

Ethics and related public policy issues in health care and biomedical research

CANCERLIT

Major cancer topics

CATLINE

Bibliographic records covering the biomedical sciences

ChemID

Dictionary of chemicals

DIRLINE

Directory of resources providing information services

DOCUSER

Directory of libraries and other information-related organizations

HealthSTAR

Clinical and non-clinical aspects of health care delivery

HISTLINE

History of medicine and related sciences

HSRPROJ

Health services research

MeSH Vocabulary

Thesaurus of biomedical-related terms

OLDMEDLINE

Citations from 1964 and 1965

PDQ

Current information on cancer treatment and clinical trials

POPLINE

Family planning, population law and policy, and primary health care

PREMEDLINE

Citations in process for MEDLINE

SDILINE

Citations from the most recent month in MEDLINE

SERLINE

Biomedical serial titles

SPACELINE

Space life sciences

TOXLINE

Toxicological, pharmacological, biochemical and physiological effects of drugs and other chemicals

TOXNET (TOXICOLOGY DATA NETWORK) DATABASES

CCRIS

Chemical carcinogens, mutagens, tumor promoters, and tumor inhibitors

DART®

Teratology. Developmental and reproductive toxicology

EMIC and EMICBACK

Mutagenicity; genotoxicity

ETICBACK

Teratology. Developmental and reproductive toxicology

GENE-TOX

Chemicals tested for mutagenicity

HSDB®

Hazardous chemicals: toxic effects, environmental fate, safety and handling

IRIS

Potentially toxic chemicals

RTECS®

Potentially toxic chemicals

TRI

Annual estimated releases of toxic chemicals to the environment

TRIFACTS

Health, ecological effects, safety, and handling information chemicals in the TRI file

B

OTHER MEDICAL AND NURSING DATABASES

The following databases are listed according to their size (number of journals or citations).

EXCERPTA MEDICA DATABASE

The Excerpta Medica Database (EMBASE) is similar to MEDLINE in size and scope. It has a particular focus on pharmacological information. Published by Elsevier Science BV in the Netherlands, the database includes approximately 3,600 journals from 1974 to the present, for a total of some 7 million citations. More than 80% of the citations have abstracts.

EMBASE is updated weekly; a total of about 400,000 citations are added each year. Like MEDLINE, it is available on CD or the Internet through a number of different software vendors.

For more information, go to ***http://www.elsevier.nl***

Or contact:

1-800-HLP-EMED
212-633-3980
E-mail: usembase-f@elsevier.com

CUMULATIVE INDEX TO NURSING AND ALLIED HEALTH LITERATURE

CINAHL (Cumulative Index to Nursing and Allied Health Literature is published by CINAHL Information Systems **http://www.cinahl.com**, a for-profit company based in Glendale, California. CINAHL focuses on issues and materials that are of specific interest to nurses and allied health professionals, making it a useful tool for these groups.

CINAHL began as a project in the 1940s and its first official publication was 1961. In 1984 CINAHL became available online, and in 1989 a CD-ROM version was released. In 1995 it became available (on a subscription basis) over the Internet. CINAHL is often available through a school or hospital, and the University of California plans to offer access to CINAHL online to all its campuses.

The CINAHL index is arranged hierarchically, similar to MeSH; it includes over 9,000 terms. CINAHL indexes roughly 1,000 nursing and allied health journals, going back to 1982. The database currently includes 250,000 articles, half of which have abstracts. Categories available for searching in CINAHL include publication types such as accreditation, CEU, teaching material, nursing diagnosis, nursing intervention, pictorial, clinical path, nurse practice acts, and standards of practice.

Perhaps the biggest weakness of CINAHL is that, unlike MEDLINE, it is not available for free on the Internet. The CINAHL database is much smaller than MEDLINE. CINAHL is stronger than MEDLINE in the subject of alternative health, including such journals as *Alternative Health Practitioner* and *Alternative Medicine Digest*. It also has a wider coverage of popular consumer health journals such as *Exceptional Parent, American Health for Women*, and *Consumer Reports on Health*. (It was discovered that the public as well as professionals were using PubMed, so it has begun to add consumer health publications to MEDLINE.)

All articles from CINAHL citations can be ordered through its document delivery service. Current price is $12 per article by mail or fax. Articles from sixteen journals can be downloaded in pdf format, for the same fee of $12 per article.

CINAHL is available on the Web as *CINAHL Direct*, but only for a fee for service. Prices are per hour of use. A block of time is purchased and can be used for one year. Current rates vary from 5 hours for $49.95 to 200 hours for $700. Student discounts are available.

The CINAHL database is also available through several third-party providers:

Data-Star	*http://www.dialog.com*
OCLC	*http://www.oclc.org*
Healthgate	*http://www.healthgate.com*
OVID	*http://www.ovid.com*
Paper Chase	*http://enterprise.bih.harvard.edu/paperchase*
Silver Platter	*http://www.silverplatter.com*

Full text of some articles published after 1994 is available, especially standards of nursing practice, articles from state nursing journals, and some consumer health information.

There is a demonstration version of CINAHL Direct on the Web. Below is the first search screen.

Search Other Fields

Tips for searching by fields

Database-CINAHL
DEMO

Search on: [_____]

Fields to Search: Enter search criteria, click on button next to desired field then ☚ Submit

○ Abstracts	○ Instrumentation	○ Month	○ Table of Contents
○ Accession Number	○ ISBN	○ Pages	○ Terms in Process
○ Author	○ ISSN	○ Publication Type	○ Text Word
○ Author Affiliation	○ Issue Number	○ References	○ Title
○ Corporate Author	○ Journal Subset	○ Serial Identifier	○ UMI Number
○ Dist/Producer Address	○ Journal Title	○ Series Title	○ Update
○ Full Journal Title	○ Language	○ Source	○ Volume
○ Full Text	○ Medline Number	○ Subject Headings	○ Year
○ Grant Information			

CINAHL search screen

After searching for a word, CINAHL offers a series of links
through a subject hierarchy.

Thesaurus

Searching the Thesaurus   Database-Demo Database

Subject *ANEMIA*

Click on appropriate subject heading below:

     BT HEMATOLOGIC-DISEASES
        LT ANEMIA
            NT ANEMIA-APLASTIC
            NT ANEMIA-HEMOLYTIC
            NT ANEMIA-HYPOCHROMIC
            NT ANEMIA-MACROCYTIC
            NT ANEMIA-NEONATAL

CINAHL thesaurus

When you make the final selection, you see a series of titles.

Display

Tips for Displaying Documents   Database-CINAHL DEMO

Search: S1: ANEMIA-SICKLE-CELL.MJX,MNX.   6 Documents

☐ A comparison study of children with sickle cell disease and their non-diseased siblings on hopelessness, depression, and perceived competence
    Abstract   Long Record
☐ Pain intensity and home pain management of children with sickle cell disease
    Abstract   Long Record
☐ Incentive spirometry and sickle-cell disease... acute chest syndrome (ACS)
    Abstract   Long Record
☐ Health and well-being ratings of African American adults with sickle cell disease: counseling service implications
    Abstract   Long Record
☐ Leg ulcers in patients with sickle cell disease
    Abstract   Long Record
☐ Pharmacology update: know the disease, understand the treatment
    Long Record

CINAHL list of article titles

And a search can be modified using fields.

Search Other Fields

Tips for searching by fields   Database-CINAHL
                                                                          DEMO

Search on: [   ]

Fields to Search: Enter search criteria, click on button next to desired field then ⬥ Submit

○ Abstracts	○ Instrumentation	○ Month	○ Table of Contents
○ Accession Number	○ ISBN	○ Pages	○ Terms in Process
○ Author	○ ISSN	○ Publication Type	○ Text Word
○ Author Affiliation	○ Issue Number	○ References	○ Title
○ Corporate Author	○ Journal Subset	○ Serial Identifier	○ UMI Number
○ Dist/Producer Address	○ Journal Title	○ Series Title	○ Update
○ Full Journal Title	○ Language	○ Source	○ Volume
○ Full Text	○ Medline Number	○ Subject Headings	○ Year
○ Grant Information			

CINAHL fields

BRITISH NURSING INDEX

The British Nursing Index (BNI) was launched January 1, 1997. It consolidates several previous databases (Nursing Bibliography, RCN Nurse ROM and Nursing and Midwifery Index) and includes approximately 220 nursing and allied health journals from 1994 to the present. Nine thousand citations are added each year. The index is compiled by librarians from the Libraries of Bournemouth University, Poole Hospital NHS Trust, Salisbury Health Care Trust and the Royal College of Nursing.

BNI is particularly strong in the areas of nursing and midwifery.

BNI is available on CD-ROM, print, or via the Internet. Individual access is by subscription; libraries in the United Kingdom may have licensing agreements.

For more information, go to

http://www.bournemouth.ac.uk/src/local/bni/bni.html

Or contact Beryl Grindrod of Bournemouth University:

bgrindro@bournemouth.ac.uk

THE COCHRANE LIBRARY

The Cochrane Library is a collaboration between the Cochrane Collaboration (an international non-profit organization) and Update Software. It was developed as a response to the call of Archie Cochrane, an epidemiologist, for systematic reviews of randomized controlled clinical studies as a way of advancing evidence-based health care.

The Library was opened in 1992 in Oxford, and the online version became available in 1998. It provides reviews, abstracts, and bibliographic information, and is available as a CD and online publication. The online version has a search function, which can be limited by title, author, abstract, keyword, date, or MeSH words. A MeSH search looks through the MeSH tree, shows the various terms, then links to results from all areas of the Library described below (CDSR, DARE, etc.). Results are given in reverse chronological order (most recent first).

The central focus of the Cochrane is on clinical trials, and the main publication of the Cochrane Library is the CDSR (Cochrane Database of Systematic Reviews) of randomized controlled trials. CDSR currently has 377 reviews of trials, and 360 reviews of protocols. CDSR reviews include the objective, search strategy, selection criteria, data collection and analysis, results, and conclusions from studies. In addition, data from multiple trials are reviewed and compared statistically.

Collaborative review groups cover areas of health care, such as Diabetes, Epilepsy, or Eyes and Vision. Within each group there are ongoing reviews of specific topics ("Antihypertensive therapy in diabetes mellitus") and protocols ("Effective coverage in schemes for diabetic retinopathy screening"). The handbook for reviewers is available online at

http://www.medlib.com/cochranehandbook

The handbook, which is several hundred pages, gives directions on writing systematic, explicit reviews; it also has extensive directions on locating trials.

The second section of the Cochrane Library is the Database of Abstracts of Reviews of Effectiveness (DARE), which currently has 366 records. This section also contains reviews from the ACP Journal Club, and about 1,200 reviews (bibliographic details only) from other sources.

The Cochrane also includes the Central, and the Cochrane Controlled Trials Register (CCTR). These are bibliographic databases with references to approximately 180,000 controlled clinical trials. The Central database is intended to be over-inclusive, whereas CCTR are those which have met quality criteria. Records in both have MEDLINE numbers and MeSH terms, when available.

Below is the main screen for the online version of the Cochrane Library, showing the various sections.

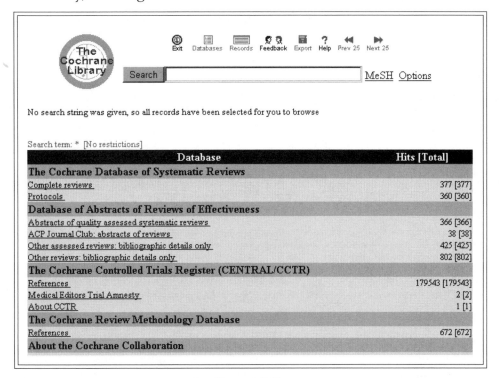

Cochrane Library

Here is a selection of the DARE reviews, showing the titles only.

1	A clinical approach for the diagnosis of diabetes mellitus: an analysis using glycosylated hemoglobin levels.
2	A comparison of the safety and efficacy of alprazolam versus other agents in the treatment of anxiety, panic, and depression: a review of the literature.
3	A critical review of studies of newborn discharge timing.
4	A literature assessment of the use of miscellaneous topical agents, growth factors, and skin equivalents for the treatment of pressure ulcers.
5	A meta-analysis of blunt cardiac trauma: ending myocardial confusion.
6	A meta-analysis of breast implants and connective tissue disease.
7	A meta-analysis of clinical studies of imipenem-cilastatin for empirically treating febrile neutropenic patients.
8	A meta-analysis of controlled trials of cardiac patient education.
9	A meta-analysis of prophylactic endoscopic sclerotherapy for esophageal varices.
10	A meta-analysis of randomized placebo control trials in fontaine stage-III and stage-IV peripheral occlusive arterial disease.
11	A meta-analysis of randomized trials comparing coronary artery bypass grafting with percutaneous transluminal coronary angioplasty in multivessel coronary artery disease.

DARE Reviews

For more information, go to

http://www.update-software.com/ccweb

or   *http://www.updateusa.com*

Versions of the online Cochrane Library are available in Spanish and German.

Email:
info@update.co.uk
updateinc@home.com
USA telephone number:
760-727-6792

RNDEX

RNdex is a bibliographic database produced and maintained by an employee-owned private company, Information Resources Group. Like CINAHL, it is available as a fee for service. RNdex focuses on the more substantive English language nursing and case management journals; for example, it does not index state nursing newsletters. RNdex is strongest in the areas of case management, critical care, and oncology. The database is an excellent source of abstracts for the case management and managed care journals, many of which are not presently indexed elsewhere.

It indexes roughly 150 journals, and uses WinSPIRS, a SilverPlatter search engine.

Searching is possible using a custom nursing thesaurus of subject headings, subheadings, identifiers, and research methods. The thesaurus contains over 10,000 terms, with selected MeSH terms as well as specific nursing and case management headings not contained in MeSH. Search features include the capability to search directly on classification headings (NANDA, NIC, NOC, DSM, etc.), names of clinical assessment tools and research instruments, and names of equipment, software, or legislation.

All RNdex products are on CD-ROM at this time. For more information, see *http://www.rndex.com* or call 800-200-6040.

A student version of Rndex containing approximately the 100 core nursing journals is available as *The Nurse's Research Library* through Delmar Publishers and many health science campus bookstores. For more information on this database, contact Delmar at 800-347-7707.

A subset of the RNdex database, covering 60 journals, is freely available for searching at *http://www.springnet.com*.

The screen below shows the results of a basic search on RNdex, using the word rehabilitation. The format in which a citation is displayed is similar to the Medline format, with two-letter field names on the left for title, author, abstract, and so on. Rndex also features a document delivery field (DD - not shown) which provides information on where to obtain full text articles and the approximate cost per document.

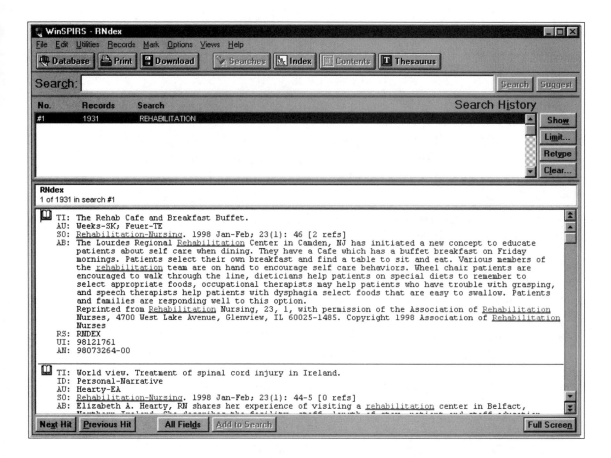

RNdex basic search

ALLIED AND ALTERNATIVE MEDICINE

Allied and Alternative Medicine (AMED) covers the fields of complementary or alternative medicine. In 1997 it expanded to include palliative care. It indexes approximately 350 journals, from 1985 to the present, and contains 90,000 citations. AMED is available online through vendors such as Datastar ***http://www.telusplanet.net/public/datastar*** or MIC-KIBIC.

Topics include:

Acupuncture
Alexander Technique
Ayurvedic Medicine
Chiropractic
Diet therapy
Healing Research
Herbalism
Holistic treatment
Homeopathy
Hypnosis
Iridology

Meditation
Moxibustion
Occupational therapy
Osteopathy
Physiotherapy
Psychotherapy
Reflexology
Rehabilitation
Traditional Chinese Medicine
Yoga

For more information, go to the Health Care Information Service of the British Library:

http://minos.bl.uk/services/sris/hcis.html

Or contact:
Medical Information Centre
British Library
Boston Spa
West Yorkshire, LS23 7BQ
UK
Telephone: +44 1937 546 039
Fax: +44 1937 546 236

C INTERNET RESOURCES

The most authoritative and up-to-date information on PubMed and MEDLINE is available directly from the National Library of Medicine, including its excellent *PubMed Training Guides*. For collected links, see the NN/LM list at **http://www.nnlm.nlm.nih.gov/nnlm/online**. This page links directly to most of the resources below.

MEDLINE LINKS

LINK LISTS

Reviews, guides, factsheets

http://www.nnlm.nlm.nih.gov/nnlm/online

Web MEDLINE sites

http://www.med.jhu.edu/peds/neonatology/ medline.html#medline

Free MEDLINE page

http://www.docnet.org.uk/drfelix

MEDLINE search sites

http://www.hudgp.org.au/medline.htm

MEDLINE resource center

http://omni.ac.uk/general-info/internet_medline.html

MEDLINE providers

http://www.mednet-i.com/html/m_line.html

PUBMED AND NLM SITES

PubMed

http://www.ncbi.nlm.nih.gov/PubMed

Internet Grateful Med

http://igm.nlm.nih.gov

National Library of Medicine

http://www.nlm.nih.gov

BRIEF OVERVIEWS AND DESCRIPTIONS OF PUBMED

FAQ: MEDLINE and MEDLARS

http://www.nlm.nih.gov/databases/medlars_faq.html

PubMed

http://www.nlm.nih.gov/pubs/factsheets/pubmed.html

PubMed Review

http://www.medlib.iupui.edu/ref/pubmed.html

MEDLINE FAQ

http://www.medlib.iupui.edu/faculty/medline-faq.html

Evaluating MEDLINE: PubMed

**http://omni.ac.uk/general-info/internet_medline/
pubmed.html**

TUTORIALS

PubMed training manuals

http://www.nlm.nih.gov/pubs/web_based.html

PubMed quick guide

http://www.mssm.edu/library/pubmed.htm

MEDLINE

http://nimnet51.nimr.mrc.ac.uk/Library/dtop/dtop02.htm

PubMed searching tips

http://www.med.mun.ca/hsl/guides/pubmed.htm

Boolean primer

**http://www.cnet.com/Resources/Tech/Advisers/Search/
search3.html**

PubMed tutorial

http://www.chu-rouen.fr/documed/pmeeng.html

MESH AND UMLS

MeSH overview

http://www.nlm.nih.gov/mesh

MeSH tree structures

http://www.nlm.nih.gov/mesh/mtrees.html

Factsheet on MeSH

http://www.nlm.nih.gov/pubs/factsheets/mesh.html

UMLS overview

http://www.nlm.nih.gov/research/umls

UMLS complete documentation

http://www.nlm.nih.gov/research/umls/UMLSDOC.HTML

DOCUMENT DELIVERY SERVICES

NLM Loansome Doc

http://www.nlm.nih.gov/pubs/factsheets/loansome_doc.html

http://www.nnlm.nlm.nih.gov/nnlm/docdel/loansome.html

**http://www.nnlm.nlm.nih.gov/nnlm/docdel/
loansome_lib.html**

Lists of document delivery services

http://www.nnlm.nlm.nih.gov/pnr/docsupp

http://www.med.virginia.edu/hs-library/outreach/med.htm

Individual services

Advanced Information Consultants

> **http://www.AdvInfoC.com**

ASAP

> **http://sun3.lib.uci.edu/~mlriweb/asap.htm**

Biomedical Information Service

> **http://www.biomed.lib.umn.edu/bishp.html**

British Library Doc. Supply Centre

> **http://www.bl.uk**

Canada Inst. for Sci. & Tech. Info.

> **http://www.nrc.ca/cisti**

Countway Express

> **http://www.countway.med.harvard.edu**

Document Center

> **http://www.doccenter.com**

EBSCO Document Services

http://www.ebscodoc.com

ExtraMed

no web site. Call +44-1730-301297 (England)

Faxon

http://www.faxon.com

Health Information for You

http://healthlinks.washington.edu/hsl/hify

Information Express

http://www.express.com

Infotrieve

http://www.infotrieve.com

ISI

http://www.isinet.com

KIWI

http://www.niwi.knaw.nl

Linda Hall Library

http://www.lhl.lib.mo.us

Michigan Info. Transfer Source

http://www.lib.umich.edu/mits

Northern Light

http://www.nlsearch.com

Rudder Library Services

http://www.rudderlibrary.com

TDI Library Services

http://www.tdico.com

UMI

http://wwwlib.umi.com/infostore

UnCover

http://uncweb.carl.org

UW

http://www.lib.washington.edu

WISE for Medicine

no web page. Call 1-800-667-9473

OTHER MEDLINE INTERFACES

Knowledge finder

http://www.kfinder.com

Ovid

http://demo.ovid.com/libpreview

Paperchase

http://www.paperchase.com

SilverPlatter

http://forge.silverplatter.com/webspirs/webspirs.htm

MISCELLANEOUS

Dewey Decimal System

http://www.oclc.org

Evaluating Web MEDLINE sites

**http://www.med.virginia.edu/~wmd4n/amia/
medline.html**

Glossary of library terms

**http://www.nnlm.nlm.nih.gov/nnlm/online/
northwoods/handout.html**

Health Science Librarians

**http://bones.med.ohio-state.edu/hsl_resources/
index.html**

BEYOND MEDLINE:
INTERNET MEDICAL RESOURCES

WHAT YOU WON'T FIND IN MEDLINE

MEDLINE is a bibliographic database with citations to medical
journals. There are some types of information that are either not in
MEDLINE, or difficult to find through a MEDLINE search alone:

- full-text articles (except for a small percentage of
  journals)
- citations to medical textbooks
- textbooks (the content)
- medical texts for purchase
- dictionaries of medical terms
- current medical news
- pharmaceutical references
- medical procedures
- patient handouts or other source material for teaching
- patient advocacy or support groups
- email and Usenet discussions on medical topics
- statistics and other epidemiological data
- addresses, phone numbers, physician listings

Most of these *are* available on the Internet, but finding them can
be difficult for a beginner.

EVALUATING INTERNET INFORMATION

You have to use judgment in assessing the quality of information
found on the Internet, because the information in these sites is
often not as reliable as that found in textbooks or established
journals. If you have questions about information on medical
sites, or how to evaluate them, take a look at these guidelines:

http://www.cmanet.org/Public_Interest/Library_of_Links/
fdacon.html

http://www.mitretek.org/hiti/showcase/documents/criteria.html

http://refserver.lib.vt.edu/libinst/critTHINK.HTM

FULL-TEXT ARTICLES

There is no single source for finding full-text articles on the
Internet, and this area of the Internet is changing very rapidly.
PubMed maintains a list of publisher sites which offer full text at
http://www.ncbi.nlm.nih.gov/PubMed/fulltext.html. Rather than
supply full text, most publishers put the table of contents on the
Web, and perhaps abstracts as well, with a few full-text articles.
Some publishers require that you subscribe before you can read
the full text of any article.

Other lists and links to medical journals which supply full text
articles on the Internet:

Electronic Journals

> *http://www.hslib.washington.edu/journals*

BioMedNet

> *http://biomednet.com*

Electronic Journals

> *http://www.mfhs.edu/library/webinfo/journal.html*

MedWeb

> *http://www.cc.emory.edu/WHSCL/medweb.html*

TEXTBOOKS

Very few medical texts (books in print) are currently available on
the Internet. One notable exception is the 16th edition (1992) of
the *Merck Manual*, which is available in Italian and Japanese as
well as English. You can find the Merck manual at:

> *http://www.merck.com*

The strength and direction of the Internet has not been in converting traditional textbooks into an electronic version, but
rather in putting up quickly changing information (such as
news) or in making large databases searchable quickly and easily.

CITATIONS TO MEDICAL TEXTS: NLM LOCATOR

telnet://locator.nlm.nih.gov

The National Library of Medicine has a free search function, called *Locator*, for texts. (A major upgrade to Locator is planned for the fall of 1998. See Appendix A for more details.) Locator accesses a group of distinct databases:

CATLINE	book catalog	over 600,000 listings
AVLINE	audiovisuals	over 22,000 listings
SERLINE	journal catalog	list of titles and call numbers
DIRLINE	organizations	over 15,000 listings

For more information on using Locator, and a link to the telnet location, go to

http://www.nlm.nih.gov/databases/locator.html

From this page you can click on the link to Locator. This uses the telnet function of the Internet, a protocol for logging into distant computers and running a program on that distant computer. (You cannot dial directly into Locator.) Telnet is a communication protocol that preceded the Web. Using telnet, you log into a distant computer and maintain a connection between both computers at all times. As you type, the keystrokes are sent to whatever program is running on the distant computer.

Locator uses the F1, F2, and F3 keys. If your computer does not have F keys, try using Esc followed by 1, 2, or 3, respectively. For more help, see

http://www.nlm.nih.gov/databases/keyprob.html

Your Web browser will probably use a separate telnet program to make the connection to Locator. On a Windows95 computer with Netscape Communicator, this will be the Microsoft Telnet program. To start Telnet manually, go to c:\windows and double-click on telnet.exe. The telnet program should be set to VT100 terminal emulation.

Locator is a menu-based program. Each screen gives you a menu with a series of choices. For each choice, a letter is highlighted (or reversed, so the letter is white with a dark background). You can make a selection by typing the highlighted letter.

When using Locator, citations can be emailed directly to yourself.

Locator has directions for every screen. Here is a brief overview:

First screen: type locator to log in (must be
                   lowercase).
Second screen: press **Escape** key (esc) twice.
Third screen: type your email address (optional).
                   Press **Enter**.

General commands in Locator:

esc-esc   Return to the previous screen
F1   Help
F2   Start over
F3   View selected item(s)
Enter   Select item
m   Email selected items to yourself

CITATIONS TO MEDICAL TEXTS: GENERAL LIBRARIES

Medical Libraries on the Web

http://www.arcade.uiowa.edu/hardin-www/hslibs.html

LIBRARY OF CONGRESS

The Library of Congress has a Web interface for searching its catalog at
http://lcweb.loc.gov/z3950/mums.html.

For a list of all libraries that are searchable via the Web, go to
http://lcweb.loc.gov/z3950.

MELVYL

Melvyl is the online system used by the University of California and California State University systems, which collectively contains 9.5 million items. Faculty, students and staff can search any database (including a Melvyl interface to MEDLINE) but the public can only search the book and periodical catalogs.

http://www.melvyl.ucop.edu

DOODY PUBLISHING

Doody Publishing is a reviewer of health science books with a listing of 35,000 books.

http://www.doody.com/dej.htm

MEDICAL TEXTS FOR PURCHASE

Medbookstore.com claims to have over 80,000 titles and guarantees a 24-hour turnaround time for delivery. The site has an easy-to-use search screen, or you can browse by category.

http://www.medbookstore.com

Login Brothers Book Company carries over 50,000 items (books and other media), searchable by keyword, subject, or publisher, or browsable by subject. Health professionals can order directly from its Web page. Login hosts the Medscape Bookstore, which includes a new book notification service and pre-publication specials.

http://www.lb.com

First Internet Medical Bookstore includes supplies and equipment, as well as books.

http://www.fimb.com

To search for general-interest books on health, I recommend one of the large online booksellers, all of which you can search by author, title, or subject.

Amazon.com

http://www.amazon.com

Barnes and Noble

http://www.barnesandnoble.com

Books.com

http://www.books.com

Bookserve

> *http://www.bookserve.com*

To find a bookstore that has books on a particular topic, search or browse the list of 4,500 independent stores provided by the American Booksellers Association:

> *http://www.bookweb.org/bookstores*

DICTIONARIES OF MEDICAL TERMS

The following are general medical dictionaries. There are also smaller dictionaries which deal with specific conditions or areas of practice.

AMA

> *http://www.ama-assn.org/insight/gen_hlth/glossary*

Chorus

> *http://chorus.rad.mcw.edu*

Mayo Health

> *http://www.mayohealth.org*

MedHelp

> *http://medhlp.netusa.net*

MedicineNet

> *http://www.medicinenet.com*

Nine-Language Dictionary

> *http://allserv.rug.ac.be/~rvdstich/eugloss/welcome.html*

Online Med Dictionary

> *http://www.graylab.ac.uk/omd*

CURRENT MEDICAL NEWS

Medical news (headline news) can be found on many different sites. Medical organizations (AMA), newspapers and media companies (CNN, LA Times), commercial medical sites, and search engines often carry health or medical news.

List of online newspapers

http://www.ecola.com/news/press

AMA

http://www.ama-assn.org

Artigen

http://www.artigen.com/newswire/health.html

CNN Health

http://www.cnn.com/HEALTH

Headline News

http://www.achoo.com/features/headlinenews

Lycos Health

http://news.lycos.com/headlines/Health

Medical Breakthroughs

http://www.ivanhoe.com

MedicineNet

http://www.medicinenet.com

NewsIndex

http://www.newsindex.com

Newspage

http://www.newspage.com

Reuters

http://www.reutershealth.com

Yahoo News (Health)

http://dailynews.yahoo.com/headlines/health

Your Health Daily

http://nytsyn.com/med

PHARMACEUTICAL REFERENCES

DrugInfoNet

http://www.druginfonet.com

HealthTouch

http://www.healthtouch.com

MedicineNet

> *http://www.medicinenet.com*

PharmInfoNet

> *http://pharminfo.com/drugdb/db_mnu.html*

RxList

> *http://www.rxlist.com*

RxMed

> *http://www.rxmed.com*

MEDICAL PROCEDURES

Diagnostic procedures

> *http://www.healthgate.com*

PATIENT HANDOUTS OR OTHER SOURCE MATERIAL

This is perhaps the fastest-growing area of health information on the Web, and likely to remain so. Most commercial medical sites now offer handouts and health information. Remember copyright issues when using this information. Healthfinder, from the federal government, is an excellent site.

AAFP

> *http://www.aafp.org/patientinfo*

Guide to sites

> *http://www.nashville.com/~health/health_2.htm*

HealthAnswers

> *http://www.healthanswers.com*

HealthFinder

> *http://www.healthfinder.gov*

HealthGate

> *http://www.healthgate.com*

InteliHealth

> *http://www.intellihealth.com*

MedHelp

> *http://medhlp.netusa.net*

National Hlth Info Center

> *http://nhic-nt.health.org*

PATIENT ADVOCACY OR SUPPORT GROUPS

CMHC

> *http://www.cmhc.com/selfhelp*

Johns Hopkins list

> *http://infonet.welch.jhu.edu/advocacy.html*

NHIC

> *http://nhic-nt.health.org*

EMAIL AND USENET DISCUSSION LISTS ON MEDICAL TOPICS

You must subscribe to a mailing list before you can participate, but subscribing is free. Many lists maintain archives on the Web. To find lists or Usenet groups:

Liszt

> *http://www.liszt.com*

Tile.net

> *http://tile.net/lists*

To search Usenet discussions for a topic:

AltaVista

> *http://www.altavista.digital.com*

DejaNews

> *http://www.dejanews.com*

STATISTICS AND OTHER EPIDEMIOLOGICAL DATA

CDC Wonder

http://wonder.cdc.gov

Links

http://www.nnlm.nlm.nih.gov/pnr/etc/pubhlth.html

Natl. Cntr. for Hlth Statistics

http://www.cdc.gov/nchswww

ADDRESSES, PHONE NUMBERS, PHYSICIAN LISTINGS

AMA Physician Select

http://www.ama-assn.org/aps/amahg.htm

Hospitals

http://www.hon.ch

HospitalWeb

http://neuro-www.mgh.harvard.edu/hospitalweb.shtml

Virtual Hospital

http://www.vh.org/Beyond/PeerReviews/04Societies.html

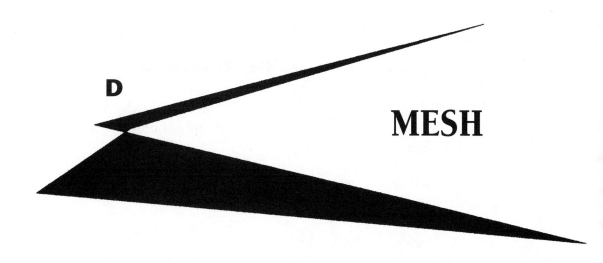

D

MESH

See Chapter 5 for a description of MeSH and an illustration of how the tree functions. Chapter 6 has exercises in using the MeSH browser.

Top of MeSH Tree
    Nervous System Diseases
        Central Nervous System Diseases
           Brain Diseases
              Cerebrovascular Disorders
                  Carotid Artery Diseases
                      Carotid Artery Thrombosis
                      Carotid Stenosis
                      Moyamoya Disease

                  Cerebral Amyloid Angiopathy
                  Cerebral Aneurysm
                  Cerebral Anoxia
                  Cerebral Arteriosclerosis
                  Cerebral Arteriovenous Malformations
                  Cerebral Artery Diseases
                  Cerebral Embolism and Thrombosis
                      Carotid Artery Thrombosis
                      Sinus Thrombosis
                      Wallenberg's Syndrome

                  Cerebral Hemorrhage
                      Hematoma, Epidural
                      Hematoma, Subdural
                      Subarachnoid Hemorrhage

Example of MeSH hierarchy

TOP LEVEL MESH STRUCTURE

These are the top-level categories in the MeSH hierarchy. Use the MeSH browser to jump to any point in the tree and/or add a term to your query.

A. Anatomy
B. Organisms
C. Diseases
D. Chemicals and Drugs
E. Analytical, Diagnostic and Therapeutic Techniques and Equipment
F. Psychiatry and Psychology
G. Biological Sciences
H. Physical Sciences
I. Anthropology, Education, Sociology and Social Phenomena
J. Technology and Food and Beverages
K. Humanities
L. Information Science
M. Persons
N. Health Care
Z. Geographical Locations

SUBHEADINGS

Subheadings are subdivisions of MeSH terms. When you show the search syntax using the Details button, the term and sub-heading are separated by a forward slash: term/subheading Thus an article may be assigned *toxemia/metabolism*, or *cervical verte-brae/radiology*.

Use the **MeSH browser's Detailed Display** to narrow a search down to the exact subject.

Following each subheading is the year it was introduced into MEDLINE. In other words, from that year forward these subheadings became available.

Abnormalities	66	Growth & Development	66
Administration & Dosage	66	History	66
Adverse Effects	66	Immunology	66
Agonists	95	Injuries	66
Analogs & Derivatives	75	Innervation	66
Analysis	67	Instrumentation	66
Anatomy & Histology	66	Isolation & Purification	66
Antagonists & Inhibitors	68	Legislation & Jurisprudence	78
Biosynthesis	66	Manpower	68
Blood	67	Metabolism	66
Blood Supply	66	Methods	75
Cerebrospinal Fluid	67	Microbiology	67
Chemical Synthesis	68	Mortality	67
Chemically Induced	67	Nursing	66
Chemistry	91	Organization &	
Classification	66	Administration	78
Congenital	66	Parasitology	75
Contraindications	91	Pathogenicity	66
Cytology	67	Pathology	66
Deficiency	75	Pharmacokinetics	88
Diagnosis	66	Pharmacology	66
Diagnostic Use	67	Physiology	66
Diet Therapy	75	Physiopathology	66
Drug Effects	66	Poisoning	66
Drug Therapy	66	Prevention & Control	66
Economics	78	Psychology	78
Education	67	Radiation Effects	66
Embryology	66	Radiography	67
Enzymology	66	Radionuclide Imaging	78
Epidemiology	66	Radiotherapy	66
Ethnology	75	Rehabilitation	67
Etiology	66	Secondary	80
Genetics	78	Secretion	68

Standards	68	Transplantation	66
Statistics & Numerical Data	89	Trends	78
Supply & Distribution	68	Ultrasonography	91
Surgery	66	Ultrastructure	75
Therapeutic Use	66	Urine	67
Therapy	66	Utilization	68
Toxicity	66	Veterinary	66
Transmission	75	Virology	95

MESH AGE GROUP TERMS

A search in PubMed can be limited to specific age groups, for example if you are looking for clinical research done with children. Type age group in the MeSH Browser to see this list (along with variations, such as *Child, Hospitalized*) and add that term to a query. For more information on the MeSH browser, see chapter 5.

Infant, Newborn	Birth to 1	month
Infant	1 – 23	months
Child, Preschool	2 – 5	years
Child	6 – 12	years
Adolescence	13 – 18	years
Adult	19 – 44	years
Middle age	45 – 64	years
Aged	65+	
Aged, 80 and over	79+	

DRUG SUBHEADINGS

These are the subheadings which can be used to limit a search related to a particular pharmaceutical. Type the name of the drug in the MeSH browser (e.g., `ampicillin`) and then click **Detailed Display** to see the subheadings.

administration and dosage
adverse effects
analogs and derivatives
analysis
antagonists and inhibitors
blood
cerebrospinal fluid
chemical synthesis
chemistry
classification
contraindications
diagnostic use
economics
history
immunology
isolation and purification
metabolism
pharmacokinetics
pharmacology
physiology
poisoning
radiation effects
standards
supply and distribution
therapeutic use
toxicity
urine

SEARCHABLE FIELDS IN PUBMED

The MEDLINE database includes the following fields which can be searched from the PubMed Advanced Search form. These are a subset of the category qualifiers. MeSH terms, publication types, and substances are particularly useful fields for searching.

Affiliation

Institution and address of primary author. These are supplied by the publisher, so they are not in a standard format, nor do all contain a zip code.

All Fields

All searchable fields.

Author Name

Author name, in the format *jones db*.

E. C. Number

Number assigned to enzymes. Field includes Chemical Abstract Service (CAS) numbers.

Journal Title

Title of the journal where the article appears. In MEDLINE, these are abbreviated. The List Terms or Journal Browser can be used to find journals.

Language

Original language of the article.

MeSH Major Topic

MeSH terms which describe the major subject(s) of an article.

MeSH Terms

Medical Subject Headings and Subheadings.

Modification Date

Date the article is entered into PubMed. Example: 1997/11/05

Page Number

First page of the article.

Publication Date

Date the article was published. Example: 1997/11/05. You can search this field by year, year/month, or year/month/day.

Publication Type

Form or type of an article, such as clinical trial, letter to the editor, or review article.

Substance

Name of chemicals from the Chemical Abstract Service (CAS) registry.

Text Words

Terms from the title, abstract, MeSH terms, and chemical substance names.

Title Words

Terms from the title of an article.

Volume

Journal volume number.

MEDLINE ID

MEDLINE identification number for an article.

PubMed ID

PubMed identification number for an article.

PUBLICATION TYPES

Articles in PubMed are classified into the following Publication Types. You can use these to limit a search to a specific kind of publication, such as a review of the literature or a clinical trial. To add a publication type to a search, use any of the Advanced Search screens. Select **Publication Type** as the field and **List Terms** as the Mode. Then type the letter a in the text box, and click **Search**.

See Chapter 4 for instructions on using the List Terms mode to apply publication types to a search.

The Review categories are especially useful. Their specific meanings are as follows:

Review	all types of review shown below
Review, academic	comprehensive, critical, or analytical review
Review, multicase	review with epidemiological applications
Review of reported cases	review of known cases of a disease
Review literature	eination of recent literature
Review tutorial	broad overview of a subject for the non-specialist or student
Scientific Integrity Review	reports from the U.S. Office of Scientific Integrity

abstract
addresses
bibliography
biography
classical article
clinical conference
clinical trial
clinical trial, phase i
clinical trial, phase ii
clinical trial, phase iii
clinical trial, phase iv
comment
consensus development
    conference
consensus development
    conference, nih

controlled clinical trial
corrected and republished
    article
dictionary
directory
duplicate publication
editorial
festschrift
guideline
historical article
interview
journal article
lectures
legal brief
letter
meeting report

meta analysis

monograph

multicenter study

news

overall

periodical index

practice guideline

published erratum

randomized controlled trial

retracted publication

retraction of publication

review

review literature

review of reported cases

review, academic

review, multicase

review, tutorial

scientific integrity review

technical report

twin study

TWO-LETTER ABBREVIATIONS (CATEGORY QUALIFIERS)

The category qualifiers are codes used by MEDLINE to name the various fields in the database. They can be used in a Boolean search. To see these codes, display the MEDLINE report for any citation.

AA	author abstract	**LA**	language
AB	abstract	**LI**	special list indicator
AD	address	**LR**	last revision date
AU	author	**MH**	MeSH headings
CA	call number	**MN**	MeSH tree number
CM	comments	**MR**	major revision date
CU	class update date	**NI**	no-author indicator
CY	country	**NM**	name of substance
DA	date of entry	**PG**	pagination
DP	date of publication	**PS**	personal name as subject
EA	english abstract indicator	**PT**	publication type
EM	entry month	**RF**	number of references
GS	gene symbol	**RN**	CAS registry number
ID	ID number	**RO**	record originator
IP	issue/part/supplement	**SB**	journal subset
IS	ISSN	**SH**	subheadings
JC	journal title code	**SI**	secondary source ID

SO	source
TA	title abbreviation
TI	title
TT	transliterated/vernacular title
UI	unique identifier
VI	volume issue
YR	year

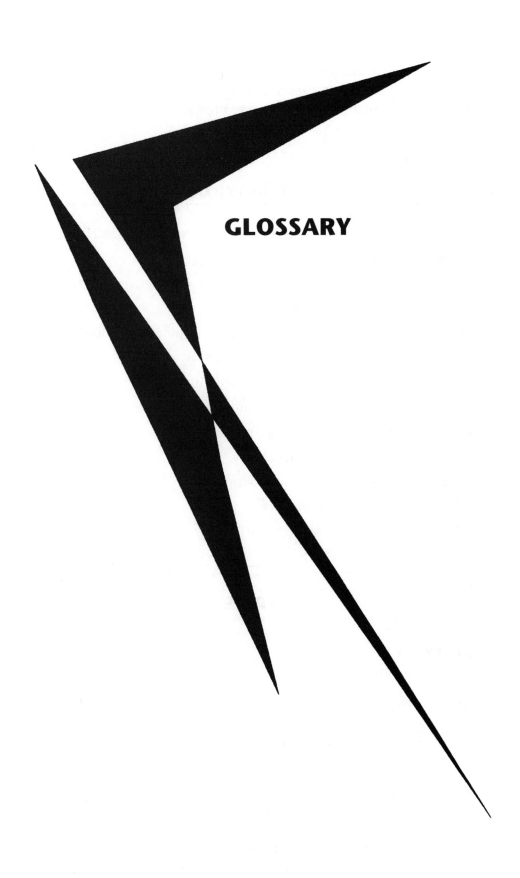

GLOSSARY

This glossary is limited to terms directly applicable to MEDLINE or library databases. It does not cover all computer topics, the Internet, informatics, or other related fields.

ABBREVIATIONS

CINAHL	Cumulative Index for Nursing and Allied Health
HTML	Hypertext Markup Language
MEDLARS	Medical Literature Analysis and Retrieval System
MESH	Medical Subject Headings
NCBI	National Center for Biotechnology Information
NIH	National Institutes of Health
NLM	National Library of Medicine
NNLM	National Network of Libraries of Medicine
OCLC	Online Computer Library Center
PDQ	Physician Data Query
PMUI	PubMed Unique Identifier
UI	Unique Identifier
UMLS	Unified Medical Language System

TERMS

ABSTRACT
  Short summary of an article.

ALGORITHM
  A formula. Each search engine uses a different algorithm to create its index. These formulas give different weight to title words, meta-tags, text, and frequency of words.

BOOLEAN LOGIC
  Use of the terms AND, OR, NOT, in formulating online search commands. Many search engines use the plus character (+) instead of AND, and the minus character (-) instead of NOT.

CALL NUMBER

The number that is assigned to a book or journal so that it can be located on the shelves of a library.

CASE SENSITIVITY

Treating capital letters differently from lower-case letters. Most search engines apply case sensitivity if a word is typed with a capital letter, but otherwise they are case-insensitive.

CATEGORY QUALIFIER

The two-letter abbreviation for fields in MEDLINE, such as AB for abstract or AU for author. See Appendix D for a list of Category Qualifiers.

CATALOGING

Assigning a number or identifier for items so that they can be physically arranged in a library. See also *classifying*.

CITATION

A reference to a particular article or book giving author, title, subject, catalog number, and keywords.

CLASSIFYING

To organize a group of items by subject, or to assign a category to each. See also *cataloging*.

CONCEPT SEARCH

A search for documents related conceptually to a word, rather than for the word itself.

DATABASE

A structured collection of information, arranged into fields. MEDLINE is a *citation* database. Hospitals use databases to track patients; businesses use them to maintain accounts and inventory.

DATABASE RECORD

The information pertaining to a single item in a database, such as the citation for one book or one article.

DECISION SUPPORT PROGRAM

A computer program which suggests alternatives or courses of action when given data. In so doing it helps to make a decision. Dr. William Detmer's DXplain, which suggests diagnoses when given symptoms, is an example of a decision support program.

DIRECTORY

A listing by category.

DYNAMIC CATEGORIZATION

Refining a search by the automatic creation of a *thesaurus* based on document themes. See AltaVista's "Refine" function for an example. Similar but not identical to the See Related Articles function in PubMed.

EXPLOSION

Expanding the subcategories beneath a term. PubMed automatically explodes MeSH terms and searches these as well as the main term.

FESTSCHRIFT

A volume of writings by different authors presented as a tribute or memorial especially to a scholar.

FIELD

A category in a database record, such as author or title. Each field contains information related to a specific aspect of the item.

FULL TEXT RETRIEVAL (OR SEARCH)

Obtaining the full body of an article or book chapter from a search, not just the citation or abstract.

FUZZY SEARCH

A search that will find matches even when words are only partially spelled or misspelled.

HIERARCHY

Ordering things or concepts by levels. A common system in medicine is that used to describe the physical body: organism, organ, tissue, cell. MeSH uses a hierarchy of concepts to organize medical concepts. See Appendix D for the top level of the MeSH hierarchy.

INDEXING

The process of compiling the index file used by a computer program to search a set of documents. Also, the process of assigning subject headings.

INFORMATICS

The study of information processing, knowledge, and data, specifically as related to computers.

KEYWORD

Word that represents one of the major concepts in a search, page, or citation.

KNOWLEDGE MAPPING

To group search results by meaning, synonyms, or related terms.

LIMIT

To restrict the number of results of a search by applying parameters. Typically done with *Boolean connectors* applied to multiple topics or specific fields. For example, limiting results to the year 1998.

MESH (MEDICAL SUBJECT HEADINGS)

The thesaurus and system of classification used by the NLM to organize and cross-reference medical literature.

META-ENGINE OR META-SEARCH

A site that links to or searches several search engines at once.

NATURAL LANGUAGE PROCESSING

The ability of a computer program to accept statements or questions phrased in common syntax, rather than a computer language, for example "How many feet are in a mile?"

NESTING

Using parentheses to create a complex search phrase. For example: (*burn* AND *infection*) NOT *staphylococcus*. Items in parentheses are evaluated first.

PHRASE SEARCH

The ability of a search engine to look for a phrase, rather than individual words. PubMed phrase searching is done by placing quotation marks around the phrase; for example, "myocardial infarction."

PROXIMITY SEARCH

The ability of a search engine to look for a word if it is near another, for example within five or ten words, or in the same paragraph. Also called adjacency search.

QUERY

A structured question that is posed using a search engine or database, typically by searching on one or more *fields*.

RANKING

The ordering of search results. In PubMed, the results of a basic search are ranked in reverse chronological order (most recent first) according to the date they were entered into MEDLINE (Entrez date). See also *relevancy ranking*.

RELEVANCY RANKING

Ordering results by how relevant they are to a word, concept, or set of pages. Relevancy is determined by an *algorithm* which is different for each search program. Results from the See Related Articles search in PubMed are ranked by relevancy.

REPORT

The format in which results of a database search or *query* are displayed on screen or printed on paper.

ROBOT

A small program used by automated search engines to look for and index new Web pages. Rough synonyms: spider, bot, worm.

SEARCH ENGINE

A program (or a site with such a program) which indexes text documents or Web pages.

SENSITIVITY

The degree to which a search or test discovers correct results (true positives). If a search has 100% sensitivity, it finds all items which fit the question. Note that it still may have false negatives, however.

SPECIFICITY

The degree to which a search or test avoids false negatives. If a search has 100% specificity, it does not turn up any false results. Note that it still may have false positives, however.

STEMMING

The ability for a search to include the stem of words, through the use of a thesaurus. For example, searching on *nursing* and also retrieving pages with the word *nurse*.

STOPWORDS

Common words which are automatically excluded from a search, such as *all, also, each, many*. PubMed has more than 350 stopwords.

THESAURUS

A list of words and synonyms. Also called controlled vocabulary. MeSH is the thesaurus for MEDLINE.

TRUNCATION

To truncate is to shorten. Using a database, truncation signifies the ability to search for a shortened form of a word, typically done with the asterisk (*). For example, searching for *card** will find cardiac, cardiopulmonary, and other words.

WILDCARD CHARACTER

A character which can stand for any other, such as the asterisk (*) used in searching on a *truncated* word.

INDEX

Topics in the following areas are grouped under the main title:

PubMed functions
MeSH
MEDLINE